Forever Just Married

SAGE RELATIONSHIP ADVICE

FROM A COUPLE WHO HAVE MADE

IT WORK FOR OVER HALF A CENTURY

FOREWORD BY
DR. MICHAEL BERNARD BECKWITH
FOUNDER AND SPIRITUAL DIRECTOR OF
AGAPE INTERNATIONAL SPIRITUAL CENTER

MARILYN AND KENT PELZ

BALBOA.
PRESS
A DIVISION OF HAY HOUSE

Balboa Press books may be ordered through booksellers or by contacting:

Balboa Press
A Division of Hay House
1663 Liberty Drive
Bloomington, IN 47403
www.balboapress.com
1 (877) 407-4847

Print information available on the last page.

ISBN: 978-1-5043-6971-8 (sc)
ISBN: 978-1-5043-6973-2 (hc)
ISBN: 978-1-5043-6972-5 (e)

Library of Congress Control Number: 2016919039

Balboa Press rev. date: 12/24/2016

To our beloved family: daughters Molly and Mindy;
grandchildren Bodhi, Jonah, Paxton, and Layla; and sons-
in-law Sequoia and Richard. We'll love you forever.

TABLE OF CONTENTS

FOREWORD

At the very center of existence there is a Presence out of which radiates a love-energy that is utterly pristine, unconditional and indestructible. Each one of us has been birthed as an individualized expression of this Cosmic Love that interpenetrates the core of our being. Is it any wonder, then, that we yearn to feel it flow through our hearts in loving exchange with one another?

On the human plane, love uniquely expresses through various forms of relationship including with the God of one's understanding, with lover, parent, child, sibling, friend, spiritual teacher, and of course with oneself. Most of us have actively engaged in several of these relationships and yet, how often have we questioned what we genuinely know about love, what we have learned as we navigate love's terrain in its multi-faceted expressions? Relationships are for relating, both to ourselves and to others. Relationship is a noun, whereas relating is a verb—it is the way in which we interact and contribute to the relationship. Have we dared to relate in a way that opens us to the challenges of going beyond our cherished notions of ourselves, beyond our expectations of others and our projections?

The book you hold in your hands is a trustworthy guide for contemplating with raw honesty where you stand as far as relating to a love relationship—whether in marriage or life partnership—as rich material to work with for your ongoing growth, development and inner awakening. After all, you are the only person you can't divorce, so isn't it worth consciously participating in relationship as a powerful vehicle for accelerating your evolutionary progress, while simultaneously offering the same opportunity to your partner? Powerful evidence to the benefits of doing so can be found in Marilyn and Kent's breakthrough discoveries in the petri dish of their own relating: "Our marriage is a laboratory where we experiment with peeling back the layers of emotional garbage to reveal the essence of who we are. This has been one of the most amazing aspects of our relationship: watching and celebrating the growth in each other. It's exhilarating beyond words. It has kept our marriage fresh, new, and interesting. Nothing less could have sustained us all these years."

What distinguishes the Pelz's work from the countless techniques described in "how-to" books on relationship is that they take us beyond what societal conditioning has taught us about committed partnership. They dare us to be honest enough, to be intimate enough with ourselves and our partners to embark on a journey from "me" to "we." In essence, they initiate readers into how to rid themselves of the troublesome ego and its projections about how a relationship should feel and look according to oneself and the outside world. By skillfully working with ego in relationship, the barrier between ourselves and other begins to dissolve, giving birth to the authentic self and therefore a relationship based upon authenticity. Authenticity then makes space for the spiritual component of relationship to emerge; it uncovers one's uniqueness as an individualized expression of Source.

Whenever I have had the privilege of counseling couples prior to conducting their marriage ceremony, I stress that if your partner says, "Never change; I love you just the way you are," it is an invitation for the relationship and the partners in it to remain stifled, stunted—the opposite of the dynamic growth potential marriage offers. Marriage is not for the faint at heart. Take for example this invitation from the authors: "See where the neurotic self makes demands to be heard, to be in charge, to state its opinion regardless of the outcome. When you see the neurotic self raising its demanding head, stop it in its tracks. This is the moment of choice you previously did not know you had." What wise counsel to begin facing what you have managed to avoid observing within yourself. As we see ourselves reflected in the mirror of relationship, we begin to release the stories we tell ourselves about ourselves including the cover ups, the rationalizations and justifications that have heretofore allowed us to avoid the inner work it takes to shift from the fictional self to the authentic self. We learn what the authors describe as using conflict to create clarity about oneself, one's partner, and the relationship you share. This in turn leads to a growing confidence and trust in relating openly, honestly, which begets genuine intimacy. Love mutually lived in such a nurturing atmosphere will unveil the beauty of each partner's soul and contribute to each other's ongoing evolutionary process.

Keep alive in your awareness the fact that love is your fundamental essence, that you are its distribution center, a passageway through which it yearns to flow. Remember that love is an ever-new relating to your partner, to yourself, to the Spirit and its energy that has drawn each of you into the magnetic field of Divine Love. Eye to eye, heart to heart, soul to soul, let Love be—as the title of this book indicates—a Forever Just Married, over and over again.

Michael Bernard Beckwith
Founder, Agape International Spiritual Center
author of Spiritual Liberation and Life Visioning

CHAPTER 1

What Is a Relationship?

Separately we are unique individuals,
but together we are a colorful creation.
—Jeffery (last name unknown), boardofwisdom.com

A relationship is not an obligation. It is not a burden. It's not an obstacle or a limitation. A relationship is a fact of life because everything is in relationship with everything else—from one corner of the universe to the other, as well as here on Earth. The highest purpose in our lives is to get relationships right—to be in harmony as much as possible with all that is. Relationships are like two dancers who are committed to improving their dance routines, moving more gracefully through life with fewer stomps on each other's toes.

For years, we thought the highest achievement was to be conscious, compassionate individuals living out purposeful lives, according to our own opinions of what was purposeful. We now know that life requires more. It takes more than just highly functional individuals (that is, individuals who are beneficial presences on the planet); there must also be highly functional couples and families and small communities and ultimately a highly functional world community. You knew life had a plan, right? We call the unfolding of that plan *evolution* (we believe life has an intention and direction, which is constantly revealing itself). None of us gets a free pass in this lifetime. Ignoring the evolutionary plan only makes our lives more difficult—some call it suffering.

From a planetary point of view, getting relationships right seems to be an imperative in this lifetime. And as the song lyric says, "let there be peace on earth, and let it begin with me," be it with our spouses, our kids, our neighbors, or others. Marriage is the perfect laboratory to hone our relationship skills. In every marriage, there are three elements: you, me, and we. Until we are willing to see that there is more than just *you* and *me*, getting to *we* can be difficult.

Ironically, it takes a really healthy *me* to be willing to transform into *we* consciousness. A healthy self-esteem is needed. Once a person has it, he or she realizes that there is nothing more to prove—no one left to impress—which makes that person eligible to become a *we*. If you already experience the *we* state of mind in your life, congratulations. You're aligning with the intention and purpose of life.

We like to think this alignment has some traction in our own relationship. Lord knows both of us have quite healthy egos. Yet neither of us feels compelled to make a move without bringing our *we* attitudes to bear. Even little things like daily household chores go better with a *we* consciousness, and for sure, our spiritual journey together has been a *we* journey.

Everything in this book points to finding *we* consciousness. We appreciate the opportunity to be your guides. As Plato once said, "The greatest privilege of a human life is to become a midwife to the awakening of the Soul in another person."

What We Believe

We believe that there is a life force creating, animating, and sustaining everything. In the macrocosm, it creates galaxies and stars and the multiverse. In the microcosm, it breathes life into us, grows our fingernails and hair, and heals our wounds. We have a choice whether to ignore this life force or to attempt to align ourselves with it; either way there are consequences. The ground rules for the game of life have already been set for us. Take gravity, for instance. We can ignore it or comply with it—both ways have consequences. Most people automatically comply with the law of gravity, but there are other laws that many people miss—for instance, the law that says that the use of force, violence, or aggression can never create peace, balance, and equanimity between nations or between two people. As Albert Einstein said, you can't solve a problem using the same thinking that created the problem in the first place. For instance, you can't use more anger to solve an argument between two people. Someone has to introduce a more accommodating energy into the conversation.

We also believe that life goes much more amicably when we pay attention to what works and doesn't work in life. Life gives us two kinds of feedback: pain and suffering and the absence of pain and suffering. We have found that we have a direct connection with the universal intelligence that will reveal the difference to us. There is no need for any intermediaries, dogmas, or spiritual practices. You climb your mountain; others climb theirs. There is only one operating principle in life, and we call it *love*. Love is the inspiration that constantly flows through all life forms, urging all of us to allow it to reveal itself through our lives. Love is the verb that sets all things in motion. When we let this love express itself through us, we experience bliss. Love is the glue that holds the universe in place. In studying and contemplating the nature of life, we gain a deep knowledge of that which created us, sustains us, and inspires us to be our highest selves. Both the scientific and spiritual paths can assist us in our journeys from ignorance to knowledge.

There is no heaven, no hell, no sin, and no judging deity that decides our fates or rewards. There is only human ignorance of the truth of how the universal works. In ignorance, we struggle and experience pain and suffering. In truth, we experience peace, harmony, and bliss.

For centuries, spiritual masters have taught that all is one. Humans are woven into the fabric of life that extends from the tiniest microcosm to the furthest corners of the universe. Yet our human experience suggests something different, and for generations, humans rationalized the world based on separateness and individuality. In the late 1800s, Newton's classical physics gave way to a new view of reality—quantum physics. The implications of this enormous scientific paradigm shift are still unfolding, including the fact that for the first time, today's greatest scientific minds are confirming what the ancient spiritual masters intuited—that man is a wave in the boundless ocean of universal consciousness.

What Is Marriage, Anyway?

Like almost everyone else in the second half of the twentieth century, we entered into marriage without a plan. If you were in love, marriage was the thing to do. Society definitely condoned it, maybe even expected and demanded it. The fact that divorce was becoming a national epidemic didn't faze us for a minute. There was no official marriage operating manual. Getting married just seemed like the right thing to do. We had never read the quote by Sydney J. Harris that says, "Almost no one is foolish enough to imagine that he automatically deserves great success in any field of activity; yet almost everyone believes that he automatically deserves success in marriage."

We eventually discovered that marriage is a lot of work; it doesn't just automatically work out for the best. They say if couples knew how much work and expense kids were, they'd never have them, and the same can probably be said about marriage—except that it's a lot harder to change your mind about being a parent after the fact.

We're not against divorce, per se, but we do think many couples give up too soon. What's more, the dysfunctional behavior patterns that caused the first marriage to fail may be carried forth into subsequent marriages. Ultimately we have to embrace and manage our own dysfunction if we want successful relationships of any kind in our lives.

Joseph Campbell, American mythologist, author of *Open Life*, and lecturer, had this to say about marriage:

> Marriage is not a love affair. A love affair has to do with immediate personal satisfaction. But marriage is an ordeal; it means yielding, time and again. That's why it's a sacrament: you give up your personal simplicity to participate in a relationship. And when you're giving, you're not giving to the other person: you're giving to the relationship. And if you realize you are in the relationship just as the other person is, then it becomes life building, a life fostering and enriching experience, not an impoverishment because you're giving to somebody else … each helping the other to flower, rather than just moving into the standard archetype. It's a wonderful moment when people can make the decision to be something quite astonishing and unexpected, rather than cookie-mold products.

Ram Dass, author and spiritual teacher, also gives us a good insight into marriage in his book *Grist for the Mill*:

> The reason you form a conscious marriage on the physical plane with a partner is in order to do the work of coming together to God. That is the only reason for marrying when you are conscious. The only reason. If you are marrying for economics, if you are marrying for passion, if you are marrying for romantic love, if you are marrying for convenience or gratification, it will pass and there will be suffering. The only marriage contract that works is what the original contract was. We enter into this contract in order to come to God together.

If this is not how you view your marriage, not to worry. It took us decades to figure out that our marriage had a higher purpose than just being good lovers, parents, and responsible members of society. Once we had agreement on the highest purpose of our marriage, everything changed. And our agreement was similar to that described by Ram Dass in the passage quoted above: we both wanted to be (1) more aware, (2) more conscious, (3) more fully functioning, (4) more spiritually fulfilled, and (5) more united as a couple, and we agreed that we would accept the feedback and coaching of one other to achieve these goals.

Once this agreement was in place, it became the relationship north that guided us in every important decision, every disagreement or argument. If Marilyn said something that hurt Kent's feelings, the question would be, "Is her comment within the spirit of the feedback and coaching that we both agreed to accept?" If yes, then his hurt feelings were his problem to resolve, not Marilyn's. If either of us was in a grumpy or disagreeable mood, then that person could ask him or herself, "Is this attitude making our relationship more workable and loving, or do I need to take responsibility for my mood and change it?"

The agreement could also be used to resolve questions such as, "Should we take a week's vacation in Hawaii or just veg out at home and do nothing?" Answer: stay home if that money could be used to attend a week-long consciousness-raising seminar instead. Right about now, you might be saying, "you guys sound boring ... or way too goody-goody for me," or something like that. Personally, we think we're pretty interesting and fun and not straight-laced at all. But more importantly, there is a key relationship principle here. Tony Robbins, motivational life coach, said it this way, "nothing tastes as good as wellness feels." In our world, we translate Tony's quote this way: no amount of self-indulgence can equal the deep satisfaction of relationship mastery. Being a *we*, is much more thrilling than being a *me*, because it aligns us with the nature and intent of the universe itself. Yes, we do believe the universe has an intention, which is to constantly be at work making better, more conscious versions of everything it creates, including humans, which are not yet a totally positive presence on the planet.

CHAPTER 2

How It All Started

When you touch a man's body, he will enjoy the moment, when you touch a man's heart he will remember it forever.
—Dixie Waters

Both of the experiences described in the quote above happened for us on the first night we met!

We met on Friday, June 2, 1961, at the Mission Hills Country Club in a suburb of Kansas City. The event was a cocelebration of Kent's friend Kenny's fortieth birthday and Marilyn's graduation from college. Kent was invited as a blind date to meet Marilyn, something Kenny and his wife, Marti, had been trying to arrange for some time. Kenny knew Marilyn because he employed Marilyn's father as the chief engineer at his manufacturing company.

Marilyn was unaware of this blind date arrangement until she and her parents were leaving home to drive to the country club. "Kenny has arranged a date for you tonight," her mother told her as nonchalantly as possible. Marilyn was surprised, since she was pinned to her college sweetheart at the time but was planning to break it off with him that weekend when she returned to Manhattan, KS, for graduation ceremonies.

Kenny and Marti had been telling Kent about Marilyn for some time, and while he had never seen a picture of her, he was looking forward to meeting her. Kent had graduated from college in 1958 and had been working in Kansas City for the last three years. He had dated around, without much luck of meeting anybody that really interested him. So he was always up for meeting someone new.

Kent can still remember what Marilyn wore that night. In those days in Kansas City, you dressed up if you were invited to one of the upscale country clubs, and Marilyn had chosen an off-the-shoulder black dress that showed off her lovely, long neck and petite shoulders. Kent was immediately attracted to her. Before the evening ended, the sparks were flying in both directions.

Even though we were out late that first night, Kent called Marilyn early the next morning to ask her for another date that evening. No luck; she was getting ready for her graduation ceremony. "How about Sunday night?" he asked. Again no luck; she wouldn't be back from Manhattan until late. So we agreed on Monday night. That was followed by another date on Tuesday evening, at which time Kent asked Marilyn to marry him, and she said yes!

For years, people have asked us how our relationship developed so quickly. We can only say that the physical and emotional attraction was the strongest thing we had ever experienced in our years of dating. It felt like the universe had lined up to bless our union; the feelings were that strong. From that moment on, our desire to consummate our love for one another moved quickly.

But first there was a slight delay. Marilyn had already made plans to take a three-month student tour of Europe, and her plans called for her to leave two weeks after we met, returning in late August, just in time to begin her first teaching job. Kent arranged to fly from Boston for a business trip and then to New York City to see Marilyn off, and we agreed to write each other every day while apart.

Marilyn's mom, Hope, wasn't so sure she could trust us. She thought Kent might try to convince Marilyn to stay home at the last minute. So Hope asked a next-door neighbor, whose husband was an airline pilot (meaning she could fly free), to accompany Marilyn to New York City and make sure she got on the plane headed for Europe. It all worked out fine, although the friend had to make herself scarce in the airport while Marilyn and Kent remained in a passionate embrace for several hours until her plane departed.

They say absence makes the heart grow fonder, and so it was in our case. Every letter expressed and expanded our growing love in a way that being together might not have accomplished. And while Kent was learning more about Marilyn each day through her letters, he was also cultivating a new nuclear family—Marilyn's mother and father. We spoke or saw each other almost daily that summer, and as the time grew near for Marilyn to return, her mother thought, *I hope Marilyn doesn't come home and decide to dump this boy, because I really like him now.* Fortunately, that didn't come to pass. (P.S. We still have all the love letters we sent each other that summer of 1961.) "It was a very good year," as composer Ervin Drake wrote and Frank Sinatra sang in 1961.

Upon reuniting, Kent presented Marilyn with an engagement ring he had purchased over the summer, and we were officially engaged. Not wanting to wait until the following summer to get married, we scheduled our wedding for the Christmas vacation break—December 28. We had a lot to do in the next four months, not least of which was arranging for Kent's parents to meet Marilyn and her parents. In retrospect, we realize we put a large burden on Marilyn's mother to plan the wedding, because we were both still in-the-clouds in love and Marilyn was starting her new teaching career. Thank goodness our two daughters didn't follow in our footsteps when they each got married.

Getting to Know Each Other

From the first day we met until the night of our wedding, Kent had never seen a mean look on Marilyn's face. He saw the first one at the wedding altar! Kent accidentally stepped on her wedding dress train while she was moving forward, and she was trying to send him a signal to step off. Right then, he knew she had a mind of her own and wasn't afraid to express it.

There is something about the passage of time that gives you perspective—especially when that time span is over fifty years. We now see that Marilyn was an early manifestation of the feminist movement, even though it would be at least another ten years before the actual bra burning began (other women's, not Marilyn's). As an only child born late in her parents' marriage, Marilyn had the full love and attention of both her father and her mother. So, while she could be every inch the lady her mother wanted her to be, she also had the intellectual self-confidence of her engineer father. There is evidence of that in her college major and teaching career—math!

Kent's 1940s childhood conditioning had been "Father knows best"; his mom had kept her opinions to herself (at least in front of her two sons). So, Kent assumed he would be the dominant one in the relationship with Marilyn. Oh, yeah! Surprise! While the transition wasn't easy, the only thing that saved Kent from this false perception, it turns out, was that he was himself an early manifestation of a SNAG (sensitive new age guy).

Right here we need to make a point. We are both proud of our Midwestern heritage and feel it instilled in us certain values that have served us well all our lives. But by the same token, it was the Midwestern satisfaction with the status quo that finally sent us west. It appeared to us that social mores have a way of discouraging people from changing. It is as if the collective opinion wants to neutralize those who attempt to march to their own drum. It's too threatening to society's strong need to homogenize human behavior.

The same can be true in a marriage relationship. People assume their partners will always be the way they were when they first married, and when they find out this is not so, resentment can erupt. So here is our first piece of advice: Celebrate change and diversity in yourself, your partner, and others. Don't hold too tightly to how things are in this moment, because life is always changing. That's what it does. *Life* is a verb, not a noun, which means it is always on the move, never static. You are a human becoming, not a human staying. Let life take you and shape you. It's an illusion to think we are in control of anything outside ourselves—especially our life partners.

Home Sweet (and Sour) Home

The first eighteen months of our marriage, we lived in an apartment, but it wasn't long before we got the itch to buy a house. As it turned out, Marilyn came with a dowry of $3,600, which she had inherited from an aunt who had passed away a few years earlier. Those funds became the down payment for the purchase of a brand new $27,500 house in Leawood, Kansas. Remember, this was 1962, so $27,500 bought a very nice home in a very nice suburb of Kansas City.

Owning our own home turned out to be a very significant launching pad for our lives together. In this home, we discovered our joint passion for gardening. In this home, we soon realized we both loved to entertain, and our place became party central for our friends and neighbors. Into this home we brought our two newborn daughters—Molly in 1967 and Mindy in 1969. In this home we mourned the early death of Marilyn's father, Russ, at age sixty-nine. The equity in this home also gave us the financial means to move to California and immediately establish ourselves in a lovely community in West Los Angeles—Pacific Palisades.

On the darker side, this home also represented Kent's unconscious desire to "be somebody," to establish Marilyn and him as worthy of social status in Kansas City society. Kent can still feel that strange urge he had to be accepted by a certain strata of the social community, hoping they would ignore his working-class background. It never came to pass, but it so consumed him that we finally had to move to California to extract ourselves from the uncomfortable situation he had created for himself in Kansas City: feeling less-than inside but acting more-than outside. He has since come to see that all humans have a very deep-seated need to be part of the clan that dates back to our primal ancestors, for whom rejection from the tribe meant literal death.

As we look back on those first nine years together in Kansas City, we see that we were innocently happy and painfully naïve (the second trait more Kent's than Marilyn's). Some powerful life lessons were on our horizon, and we never saw them coming. Like the classic "hero's journey," these lessons toughened us up and dissolved some of our naïveté. Navigating through those choppy waters is what the rest of this book is about.

From *You* and *Me* to *We*

Take everything you read in this book with a grain of salt. Try it on for size; see if it fits. Use what works, and ignore the rest. If we've learned anything in life it's that no two people see things the same way, and what works for us might not work for you. Life is not only messy; it is also unique. The same events, circumstances, and persons are never duplicated. All of life is one of a kind—every moment for the last thirteen billion years! So any advice others offer you comes strictly from their experience and perspective and may not fit your circumstances. Life may not come with an operating manual, but there are lots of indications about what makes a successful life. For instance, if the world is one, then there is no you and me—*we* is one! Everything is in relationship with everything else. *Everything!* No exceptions. No matter how much humans struggle for their independence, freedom, and self-governance, it's not possible to have it your way all the time. We are not the center of the universe. This life is not all about us. We have to get some perspective and stop objecting to what is. Resistance has no value (e.g. war cannot create peace). Instead of resisting "evil," dance with life; don't try to control it or lead it. (Imagine a surfer trying to control the waves of the ocean, instead of just going with them.) Every relationship in our lives—casual or significant—is there to teach us something.

We have found that it helps to practice being a silent observer. We are more than neurotic, narcissistic little egos that go through life saying, "Look at me! Look at me!" or "Don't look at me! Don't look at me!" We are pure awareness, infinite consciousness that supersedes this little blip on the radar screen that we call our human experience. So be more neutral and detached about things. Observe before you act. There might be a better way. Do as your parents admonished: count to ten before you speak. Be a better listener. Be more obedient to the ebb and flow of life. Anything less causes pain and suffering.

Testing the Tensile Strength of Our Marriage

Making a commitment to one person in a marriage ceremony does not necessarily make your sexual attractions to others go away. We were married only two or three years when we discovered we could both still be attracted to someone of the opposite sex. How we handled this discovery was an important milestone in our marriage. The fact that we were both having these feelings—and discussed it with each other—went a long way toward allowing us to survive what otherwise could have been a deal-breaker. After reading *Open Marriage* by Nena and George O'Neill, we decided to pursue these feelings rather than suppressing them. This worked for about a year, after which it became clear that such an arrangement was not sustainable. A committed relationship is about more than sex. So we decided there would be *no secrets*; we confessed all our transgressions to each other in our tenth year of marriage. This definitely tested the strength of our marriage bond. Kent, especially, had some confessing to do about infidelities he had committed on business trips out of town. But Marilyn had some confessing to do, too.

CHAPTER 3

Moving to California

... the human potential and psychotherapy movements, as well as the more "life-affirming" New Religious Movements and religions of the self. This was the complex world of the Californian "psychobabble," of Scientology and Erhard Seminars Training, of Encounter Groups, meditation techniques and self-help manuals designed to assist individuals "realize their potential."
—Jamie Cresswell and Bryan Wilson

We moved to California in the summer of 1970 and landed right in the middle of the burgeoning "Human Potential" movement. Everyone was experimenting with new ways of being. We soon joined in! Marijuana. Open marriage. Encounter groups. Nude group dancing. Gregarious lifestyles. Out with the old restrictive morality, and in with the new—whatever that meant.

Through the Newcomers Club in Pacific Palisades, we met a number of young professionals who were at the same stage of family development as we were: doctors, psychiatrists, movie industry types, stock brokers, salesmen, and more. We were all going for the brass ring, California style. We may still have been trying to keep up with the Joneses, but the California Joneses were 180 degrees different from the Kansas City Joneses. It wasn't your bloodline that counted; it was your chutzpa. This was Hollywood, after all, and improv(e) was the flavor of the day.

Before leaving Kansas City, Kent read an article in the Wall Street Journal about an advertising guy who worked in downtown Los Angeles and decided to buy a home in Malibu (which was thought to be a long drive away from the city in those days). He was the west coast version of Madison Avenue advertising executives who commuted from Connecticut. After one year in our home in Pacific Palisades, we moved to Malibu, where we stayed in the same house for thirty years. It was one of the best decisions (financial and otherwise) we ever made. We bought the house for five figures in 1971 and sold it for seven figures in 2001. Our growing equity in this house allowed us to live beyond our means for almost thirty years.

Our initial freewheeling lifestyle in California lasted for about two years, allowing us to satisfy our urge to break the rules, rebel, let off steam—whatever you want to call it. While we may not have known it at the time, these early shenanigans were the seeds (and fertilizer) of what we now call our spiritual journey. It may not have looked very spiritual at the time, but what we called then the Human Potential movement, we now call the New Thought or Ancient Wisdom movement.

In 1972 we were introduced to a human potential group called Creative Initiative Foundation headquartered in Palo Alto and spreading to other major cities in California. It was a nondenominational, omnifaith movement based on the teachings of Jesus as interpreted by Dr. Henry Burton Sharman, a Canadian who authored a book called *Jesus as Teacher*. Sharman was a theologian and scientist who had studied at the University of Chicago in the first decade of the twentieth century. His book was an attempt to distill the essence of the teachings of Jesus from the additions that had been added to the New Testament along the way.

A Stanford University professor and his wife, Harry and Emilia Rathbun, were students of Sharman, leading to the establishment of study groups in the Palo Alto area in the 1950s and '60s. These study groups later became the Creative Initiative Foundation. We discovered Creative Initiative in 1972 and began taking weekly courses called The Quest for Meaning, Challenge to Change, and The Challenge of Time. These weekly courses were followed by one-week seminars each summer in a retreat facility in Ben Lomond, CA, which Creative Initiative members had built with their own hands. Our lives began to change dramatically!

Finding Our Own Spiritual Identities

We had both been raised Protestant Christians. We were married in an Episcopal church in Kansas City and established a membership in an Episcopal church in Pacific Palisades when we moved to California. But it wasn't long before our study of *Jesus as Teacher* (the great example, not the great exception) led us to rethink our Christian affiliation. Critical study of the New Testament led by Harry Rathbun and supported by writings of Christian biblical scholars made our transition easy. Rather than simply rejecting the traditional Christian Jesus who sat at the right hand of god, we found a more enlightened and relatable Jesus who walked the earth and had some personal experiences that are still relevant to our lives today.

Without the Christian structure and dogma, we were on our own to re-create our own spiritual beliefs, replacing those that we had been born into and accepted by default. Here's another piece of advice: don't believe everything your mind thinks, because those thoughts were "programmed" into you by others at an early age before you had your own power of discernment. In our current work as spiritual counselors, we have encountered numerous Catholics, Protestants, and Jews who are still looking for their spiritual paths.

Virtually every human being has been programmed by his or her parents and other authority figures. As young children, we are taught that the world can be unfriendly and that we need to prepare ourselves by creating a defensive mechanism to guard against anything painful or unpleasant. "Hot buttons" are installed that act as signals to alert us when someone or something is getting through our defenses. Think of it as going through life wearing a suit of armor. The minute you try to relate with another person, it's as if you both are wearing suits of armor and yet are trying to be gracefully in synch. It's awkward at best and often messy. Defensive systems are not 100 percent bulletproof. Hot buttons do get pushed.

We were blessed. We pushed very few of each other's hot buttons in the early years of our marriage. When it did get problematic, we had some psychological tools at our disposal, one being the "projection" theories of Carl Jung. He said, "Everything that irritates us about others can lead us to an understanding of ourselves." Ralph Waldo Emerson added that "people seem not to see that their opinion of the world is also a confession of character."

We got it! Even though we pushed each other's hot buttons, we hadn't installed them, and therefore we were not responsible for the reactions they caused. If one of Kent's buttons goes off, it's his problem, not Marilyn's. One hundred percent of the time. End of story! No matter how mad you are or how sure you are that the other person is to blame, it's your problem—pure and simple. And you can resolve it without involving the other person. We can point to several good observations on this whole subject of projection and blame:

- Byron Katie tells us that "nothing anyone else does is any of your business."
- Carl Jung says that projection doesn't actually rid you of your shadow side; rather it indicates you are in pain and need to take ownership for your projection.
- Eckhart Tolle claims that your hot button is attached to an unpleasant past experience that you are storing in your body. If another pushes your button, it's only making you recall an unpleasant experience you would prefer to forget. You're mad because the other person has activated the previous pain still stored in your body, so you lash out in retaliation.
- Our view is that every circumstance in life is a neutral event. Only humans give them value, based on their own belief systems.

We talk more about this later in the book. Right now we want to relate this to our religious metamorphosis from having an external Christian belief system to having our own internally defined spiritual belief system. When this all started—about a dozen years into our marriage—it proved to be an ideal time for us to redefine what our marriage relationship meant to us and what our vision was for our marriage. Today, when Marilyn conducts a wedding ceremony, she makes a big point of this.

Consider this: we are spiritual beings having a human incarnation, or said another way, we are eternal souls that have finite bodies to navigate through the life of form on this planet at this time. Stick with us here. We know this is a little heady, but ...

There seems to be pretty general agreement that the universe that we live in is a uni-verse—that it is *one*—and that all things are interrelated and interconnected. Everything is an expression of the one original intelligence that set everything into motion and remains involved guiding the evolution of everything it created. Chief Seattle said it this way: "Humankind has not woven the web of life. We are but one thread within it. Whatever we do to the web, we do to ourselves. All things are bound together. All things connect."

So, knowing this, we asked ourselves those ubiquitous questions: Who am I? What is our purpose—individually and collectively? We decided our purpose in life was to expand into a higher state of consciousness, thus becoming a greater expression of the Creator/Source that thought us into existence (metaphysically, not anthropomorphically) and that still resides in each of us.

Can an individual become the highest expression of his or her higher self without a marriage partner? Absolutely! Think of Jesus, Buddha, Mother Teresa, Saint Teresa of Avila, or Saint John of the Cross, to name a few. Is it easier to do it with a committed partner? We think so.

Once we decided that our primary goal was to achieve greater awareness together, it made our relationship easier. Now we had a contract to which we could refer anytime things got rough. We would simply ask ourselves, is this situation/challenge supporting our common goal to go to God together? If not, what needs to change? You could say a corporation's goal is to make a profit and every action taken and every decision made should measure up to the question *Will this action result in greater profit for the corporation … or not?*

As we're writing about this now, it all seems very clear-cut and straightforward. It was not! It took time, and there were lots of curves in the road. There were dead ends and turnabouts. But once the overarching decision was made, getting back on track was easier.

Does this mean that we don't have other goals, such as making money, dining out at fine restaurants, or shopping at Nordstrom. No, but it does mean we are more detached from these goals, not dependent on them for our happiness. (See the chapter on "Working from the Inside Out").

In It for Good (God)

We decided in the mid-'70s that we were in our marriage relationship forever, no outs. No matter how tough things might get, we wouldn't give up on the *we* we had created. We were willing to give *in* but not give *up*. It's amazing what you will do to make things better when you won't allow yourself the option to quit. We had known such good times together that there was no way we could imagine it could ever be so bad that we would want to give up on the idea that it could always be that good (and for the most part, it has been so).

There is something that dies when a commitment this binding is made. The "little self" dies. The *me* attitude dies. It turns out this kind of commitment was also good practice for another commitment we were to make: committing to live a life of high consciousness about how God/Source/Cosmic Intelligence works in our lives, to wake up from the mediocre collective culture haze. Everyone wonders what a life of higher consciousness might be all about; few take the time to seriously investigate the question.

We believe the objective of life is to be constantly gaining higher consciousness, greater clarity, and greater self-knowledge. Socrates said it 2,400 years ago: "Above all, know thyself." Elsewhere in this book, we talk about the fruitlessness of seeking the approval of others and depending on other people, circumstances, or possessions for one's sense of self-worth. These people and things are all finite and cannot give you the permanent happiness you are seeking. Life is about moving past the little self to the larger intention of universal consciousness.

It takes time to build a great relationship. Be open to new things. Learning is life-long. Talk to your partner the same way you would write in a personal diary. Be real, no more anger, judgment, or blame. The blame game gets old and is totally useless. Watch yourself for any little snipping back and forth—it's a form of close-mindedness, resentment, and unwillingness to capitulate. Do you want to be right or do you want to be in relationship? Control over others is an illusion; when we discovered this, we quit trying—or mostly, Kent quit trying. His pace through life is more hurried than Marilyn's, so almost every time we would get ready to go out, Kent would be ready to go while Marilyn was still getting ready. Not the patient type, Kent would manage to send Marilyn "nudge" signals that irritated her, momentarily spoiling our relationship and getting our evening off on the wrong foot. This would continue in the car, since now Kent was driving too fast because he thought we were now running late. Of course, we would still get to our destination on time, proving that all of Kent's impulsiveness was unnecessary. Obviously he had a neurotic issue around time, which he learned from his dad, who did the same thing to his wife. While better, Kent is still working on his impatience.

Let go and remember that all events in life truly are neutral and only humans give them a positive or negative value. Just surrender to the Universal Source that wants to express itself through you as you. At first it feels like we are putting ourselves back under the subjugation of our parents, and nobody wants to go back to that situation. But it's not. We are putting ourselves under a higher authority that loves and supports us unconditionally. What could be better than that?

A Fish out of Water

Learning something new begins with cognitive dissonance,[1] also known as "a whack on the side of the head." A full cup can receive no more water. If you are going to learn anything, you need to find a way around what you think you already know. Our wish is that *this book will disturb you!*

If you asked a fish what it was like to spend an entire lifetime in water, it would be hard-pressed to even understand what you were talking about. Ask yourself a similar question: "What's it like to live an entire lifetime totally submerged in air?" The question almost seems irrelevant, since you've probably never experienced anything else.

That's the physical world, and there is also a mental equivalent. We are all totally immersed in a collective consciousness: a collection of agreements, beliefs, and values that operate at a very deep subconscious level in every human psyche. This collective consciousness dictates how we behave toward each other as social animals—things like how close to stand next to another person, how long to look into another person's eyes, how long to hold another person in a hug, how to show respect for one another, or when to be aggressive and when to be submissive. The list is endless.

The problem is, like the fish in water, we are often not aware of how all-pervasive these collective agreements are. We take them for granted. We willingly comply with them. We have a love/hate

---

[1] People tend to seek consistency in their beliefs and perceptions. So what happens when we come across a new belief that conflicts with a currently held belief? The term cognitive dissonance is used to describe the feeling of disorientation that results from holding two conflicting beliefs. When there is a discrepancy between beliefs and behaviors, something must change in order to eliminate or reduce the dissonance.

relationship with them. They can make us feel included or left out. Genetically, we are social animals, and we want to fit in, often by compromising our own individual instincts.

Yet, just as there were fish that migrated to the land and became reptiles, there are also people who learn how to go it alone, extracting themselves from the collective consciousness. We call them people who march to the beat of their own drummers. These people may be few and far between, but there are and have been enough of them to convince us that it is possible and perhaps representative of the evolutionary direction of the human race.

What does this have to do with relationships? you might ask. We're not suggesting you need to become a Buddha, Jesus, or Gandhi to have successful relationships. However, we are asking you to consider the possibility that you don't always think for yourself; *the collective consciousness is doing your thinking for you.* Your beliefs and expectations are already hard-wired into your brain, based on your particular social conditioning, and they are dictating how you respond every moment of your life.

What is the nature of this collective consciousness in which we are all submerged? We believe it includes the beliefs that

- we live in an unsafe world;
- the stick is more powerful than the carrot; and
- in case of emergency, you should look out for yourself first.

Given these conditions, how can two people ever form a completely loving, trusting, intimate relationship? *By marching to the beat of their own drummer!* As hard as it was for the fish to live on land and take oxygen from the air, it's almost equally hard for you to suspend all your previously held beliefs about how to survive in the world in order to create a relationship with another human being who also wants to make this incredible transition from the darkness to the light. It's time to empty our cups full of false opinions and step into the field of unknowing, where all learning takes place.

All Relationships Are Do-It-Yourself Projects

You may have obtained this book thinking it was all about how to shape, push, and cajole others into being the kind of relationship partners you seek (and deserve). Sorry to disappoint, but this is a book about *you*, and only you. Being in a workable relationship is a one person job—yours! Yes, we are writing about our fifty-plus-year relationship and what's made it so much darn fun and so fulfilling, but if you read carefully, you will realize that what we are saying is that any time we fell into the trap of expecting one another to change (which we did often and sometimes still do), we quickly attempted to turn that expectation or judgment around and take full ownership of it ourselves.

Oh, these words are so easy to write and so hard to do. You have to swallow your pride, admit you're wrong, give up the need to be right, let the other person win, feel like you're selling yourself out and becoming a doormat, and completely lose who you think you are. Well, you have to make a choice. At some time or other, we have both felt these deep emotions as we tried to "walk our talk" and take full responsibility for ending the power struggle we were engaged in.

Here's how author Russ von Hoelscher expressed it: "Don't rush into any kind of relationship. Work on yourself. Feel yourself, experience yourself and love yourself. Do this first and you will soon attract that special loving other." He also said, "Before we can have a successful relationship with anyone, we first need a perfect personal relationship."

So that's what we're writing about—how to be in loving relationship with yourself and how you can share that love with someone by your side. It can double the growth—and the fun. We have never lost sight of how privileged we are to be able to share each other's journeys, to watch them unfold, and to provide commentary along the way. We really resonate with the poet Roy Croft's words, "I love you not because of who you are, but because of who I am when I am with you."

We mediate, read spiritual literature, and dialogue every morning for an hour or more. When we both worked and were raising kids, the time was thirty minutes, and we had to get up by 5:00 a.m. to make it happen. During this time, we compared notes and asked questions about how our higher selves were revealing themselves. One of our favorite sayings is, "the environment dictates the nature of the change," meaning, for instance, that when amphibious creatures moved onto land, they had to learn how to extract oxygen from air rather than from water. The new environment dictated that change. If you want to become a nurse, you enroll in nursing school. If you want to have a workable relationship, you have to enroll in relationship school, not just turn on TV to escape, when you have some work to do on your relationship.

Our unawakened selves seem to favor the negative, the bad news, the flaws, hence the success of mass media. But if you want an intimate, committed, loving relationship with a life partner, you have to shift away from this habit and look for the good in each other. As Wayne Dyer suggests, "Problems in relationship occur because each person is concentrating on what is missing in the other person." This is no surprise when you study the research of child psychologists, who report that when we are growing up, our parents tell us what we're doing wrong many more times than they tell us what we're doing right (more on this in chapter 5).

Do we lack qualities that the other wishes were present? Yes! It is a deal-breaker? No! Can this lemon be turned into lemonade? Yes!

Here's some good advice from Arielle Ford's book *Wabi Sabi Love: The Ancient Art of Finding Perfect Love in Imperfect Relationships*:

> What is Wabi Sabi? It is an ancient Japanese art form that honors all things old, weathered, worn, imperfect, and impermanent by finding the beauty in the imperfections. For instance, if you had a large vase with a big crack down the middle of it, a Japanese art museum would put the vase on a pedestal and shine a light on the crack, or they might fill the crack with 24k gold!
>
> Wabi Sabi Love occurs when we shift our perception so that we can embrace and find the beauty and perfection in each other's imperfections, thus "going from annoyed to enjoyed"! In other words, all imperfections are perfect.

In our years together, we have had plenty of opportunities to see each other's imperfections. We've come to the conclusion that the only approach to improving our relationship is to remember that we are only as good as we think we are. So, we focus on the good stuff in each other, celebrate it, and expect more of that to show up. And so it does! You get what you expect.

You also get what you give. The reason for entering into a relationship is to give, not get. These two principles may sound contradictory. Are we supposed to enter into a relationship with expectations or not? you might ask. Yes, but you need to clarify what your expectations are. We're not talking about expecting the other to clean the house, wash the dishes, take out the garbage, and so on. Neither are we talking about expecting our partners to heal our unhealed wounds from childhood.

What we're talking about is expecting to find God in the other. Namaste—*the God in me acknowledges the God in you.* If you let your relationship unfold at the unconscious level of the world around you, you will experience a mixture of pain and pleasure, always seeking something better but finding it only temporarily. But if you choose to commit your relationship to revealing higher levels of possibilities, you will experience excitement, growth, and fulfillment.

If this is not what your relationship looks like at the moment, we suggest you do what Gandhi recommended: "Be the change you want to see in the world." We would say "be the change you want to see in your relationship," which brings us back to why all relationships are do-it-yourself projects.

CHAPTER 4

Back to the Beginning

It's never too late to be who you might have been.
—George Eliot

Whatever your current age, you have spent years refining your survival strategies—those behaviors that you absolutely believe you need to avoid pain, rejection, judgment, or control. When Kent was finally ready to reinvent himself, he went all the way back to the beginnings of his life to identify uninformed decisions made as a child that he now wanted to change. He found out it's never too late to have a happy childhood. He changed the dismissive attitude he held toward his mother (now deceased) to one of love and gratitude for who she was, and he finally understood why she wasn't more of who he wanted her to be. She was exactly the way God wanted her to be as Kent's mother.

He was coming home to the self he was before puberty—innocent, curious, open, teachable, in a state of awe and wonder, trusting, and in love with life. The master teacher, Jesus, said "Except you become as little children, you shall not enter into the Kingdom of God." We take this to mean that adult minds are not as open and receptive as the minds of children to allowing in the unconditional love and support of a benevolent universe. We have become fearful, habitual, defensive, and too sophisticated for our own good.

We recently heard on NPR that until children go through puberty, their brain frequencies are Alpha, not Beta, as most adults are. Beta is the highest frequency, and it supports all the brain's highest cognitive functions. The next is Alpha, which is the frequency master meditators vibrate at, as do other adults when they first fall asleep or wake up. That's why Deepak Chopra suggests that new meditators "RPM"—that is, rise, pee, and meditate before their brains kick into Beta. (Incidentally, below the Alpha frequency are Delta, or the dream state, and Theta, which is deep rest.)

Coming full circle from jaded adult to enlightened child is the main theme of the hero's journey, as found in the stories about King Arthur, Jesus, and Buddha and in those of fictional movie characters, such as Shrek and Batman. This achievement is reached by balancing the material and spiritual. You become more comfortable and competent in both the inner and outer worlds.

Joseph Campbell, in his book *The Hero's Journey*, says there are twelve steps to an archetypal life journey:

1. Ordinary World: The hero's normal life at the start of the story, before the adventure begins.
2. Call to Adventure: The hero is faced with something that makes him or her begin the adventure. This might be a problem or a challenge he or she needs to overcome.
3. Refusal of the Call: The hero attempts to refuse the adventure because he or she is afraid.
4. Meeting with the Mentor: The hero encounters someone who can offer advice and ready him or her for the journey ahead.

5. Crossing the First Threshold: The hero leaves his or her ordinary world for the first time and crosses the threshold into adventure.

6. Tests, Allies, Enemies: The hero learns the rules of this new world. During this time, he or she endures tests of strength of will, meets friends, and comes face to face with foes.

7. New Approach: Setbacks occur, sometimes causing the hero to try a new approach or adopt new ideas.

8. Ordeal: The hero experiences a major hurdle or obstacle, such as a life-or-death crisis.

9. Reward: After surviving death, the hero earns his or her reward or accomplishes his or her goal.

10. The Road Back: The hero begins the journey back to his or her ordinary life.

11. Resurrection Hero: The hero faces a final test wherein everything is at stake and he or she must use everything learned up to this point.

12. Return with Elixir: The hero brings his knowledge, or the "elixir," back to the ordinary world, where he or she applies it to help all who remain there.

Your life may not look exactly like this, but it is an archetype that many people have experienced. All life experiences are grist for the mill. In the old hero's journey paradigm, there were (and still are) lots of drama and challenges, all of which were overcome with focus and determination. The new hero's journey paradigm is and will be different. There is no need to challenge anything or object to anything. Just hold whatever is going on in your life lightly. Life may be calling you to your own hero's journey. Just go with it. We think we have, and the adventure has been thrilling—both positively and negatively.

Life is like a stream; it is flowing in one direction, and only when we give in to that direction do we become aware that we don't need to put in so much effort. This has sweetened our relationship, turning it into a graceful dance with lots of appreciation for each other. We are two best friends having the best time of our lives.

Finding Common Ground

We have a lot in common. Our energy levels are similar (high!). We both like to remain busy and productive. We both love people and enjoy being with friends and our spiritual community. We like to entertain, garden, eat out. We meditate together every morning and read spiritually inspiring material to each other. Our taste in home decor is similar. In fact, when we take an inventory of what we both like and don't like, there are not many places where we do not line up.

The point of telling you this is that we suggest people in relationships take an inventory of what they like and don't like. If there are not many connection points, then this has to be managed. Not every relationship looks like ours, but every relationship needs conscious evaluation on the part of both partners, with an agreement that you will find a balance of what works for you together and what requires separate time. For example, if you love to bowl and your partner doesn't, you'll go bowling with friends as necessary to fill your need while your partner does something else he or she will enjoy.

Good relationships don't just happen; they need planning and active management. For instance, you might ask yourself, what's the purpose of our relationship? Sex? Friendship? Economics? Procreation? While having kids was very high on our list—and very satisfying—our ultimate purpose was to become more conscious human beings together (which, among other things, made us better parents). We wanted to help each other uncover and resolve the hidden habits that were counterproductive to our walks through life. Our marriage is a laboratory where we experiment with peeling back the layers of emotional garbage to reveal the essence of who we are. This has been one of the most amazing aspects of our relationship: watching and celebrating the growth in each other. It's exhilarating beyond words. It has kept our marriage fresh, new, and interesting. Nothing less could have sustained us all these years.

After living many years away from Kent's home state of Illinois, we decided to return for his fortieth high school reunion. His schoolmates were all amazed to learn he'd stayed married to one wife all those years. He had been voted the biggest flirt of his class, and they were sure he would run through wives the same way he ran through girlfriends in high school. His response to them was, "Yes, I've been married more than once, but always to the same woman—a woman who was capable of reinventing herself, keeping me constantly attracted to her."

Be Best Friends

For our entire married life, we have been each other's best friends. We'd rather hang out with each other than with anyone else. No "guy time" or "girlfriend time" away from each other has ever been necessary. We entertain and amuse each other, we respect each other, and we prefer to take new adventures with each other. We have continued to find each other fascinating. We both like to grow, expand, and renew ourselves. We never find each other boring.

It's been our observation that, ironically, some best friends have fewer disagreements than married partners. Best friends resonate with what they like about each other and never ask the other to fix him or herself. Spouses, on the other hand, can look for the disagreeable behaviors they want the other to change. Somewhere early in our marriage, the deep connection between us took on the nature of best friends with benefits. We had tons of things in common. We found each other extremely interesting, and our first choice was to be with each other, rather than with our guy or gal friends. Marilyn, while she had always been a natural "gal's gal," found that she lost interest in the typical superficial gal talk and preferred to have meaningful talks about relationships with Kent. We were in the process of moving from *you* and *me* to *we*. Think about the qualities that constitute best friends' relationships and see if they are present in your marriage:

- You respect each other.
- You trust each other with your most intimate thoughts, knowing they won't be used against you later.
- You look to each other for advice and counsel.
- You are each other's biggest fans, believing in the other sometimes more than you believe in yourself.
- You share and celebrate each other's wins.
- You never talk behind each other's backs.
- You know you each have separate lives, but you're not jealous or envious of the other's activities
- You will sometimes disagree and maybe even hurt each other's feelings, but there is a mutual understanding that you will work it out … or drop it. Best friends rarely get "divorced," while over 50 percent of all marriages terminate in divorce.

So what does being best friends in a marriage relationship feel like? It feels like *we* instead of *you* and *me*. It means you move through life in tandem. Decisions, activities, significant purchases, and so on, are made or done in unison. At this point in our lives, we are apart only a few hours a week, and that's usually when Kent runs to the supermarket while Marilyn is tutoring a math student or counseling a spiritual client. For this to work, we have to agree almost 100 percent on how to spend our time. And when there is disagreement, a compromise must be found or one or the other of must capitulate to the other's preferences. But that capitulation can't be made with the sense of being a martyr or victim. If those feelings arise, you're back in the *me* instead of the *we*.

We believe finding more *we* experiences in our lives is very important for one main reason: the evolutionary direction of the universe is demanding it. For instance, there are things that do not work, such as using violence to attempt to create peace, teaching from the top down rather than from the individual up, or incarcerating without rehabilitating. Maybe even the current marriage paradigm isn't working, since 50 percent of marriages fail. Or perhaps we're using old marriage models to try to save our marriages rather than thinking about what a marriage of higher consciousness might look like.

Every moment of life is a new moment. Everything in the world changes. Stay light on your feet. Stay open at the top. Consider the possibility that everything you know about marriage is based on what your parents' marriage was like. If a new, higher-level paradigm for marriage is emerging, be willing to go with it.

Be Compassionate

Compassion is the outcome of fully realizing that we are all the same because we all come from the same creative intelligence, the same universal source. We say that as scientifically as possible, not religiously. Based on current human knowledge, it seems self-evident that the entire universe began from one huge creative expression that continues to this day. You can call it God, you can call it consciousness, or you can call it random, but all life comes from the same source, the same intelligence. No two snowflakes are the same in appearance, but they are all made of crystallized water. No two humans appear or act the same on the surface, but we all are made of the same flesh and bones and have the same survival instincts.

Next time you have a conflict with your spouse, boss, neighbor, or friend, ask yourself what's really going on. Is there a hurt child within that is conflicting with your external, unfilled needs? You both have needs and expectations, but neither is getting what he or she wants. Now ask yourself how, if we all have the same human nature, you could shift the dynamics in this conflict. Remind yourself that we're all humans struggling to get by. We all have needs, we all hurt, and we're all a little (or a lot) dysfunctional ... even neurotic. This is where compassion comes in.

We believe that compassion is the highest human virtue. The Dalai Lama's daily practice is compassion. Pema Chodron teaches (and this is paraphrased) that when you are stuck in an emotion, you should say to yourself, "May I be free of struggling." Then add, "May you be free of struggling. May all beings be free of struggling." This prayer or affirmation does several things:

- It allows you to resolve the issue you are struggling with.
- It affirms that you wish that the other person, too, be free of this struggling. (If we're all the same, then you know the other person struggles with the same issues you do.)
- It wishes the same well-being for all people on the planet.

Imagine what life on this planet would be if, as we resolved our strugglings personally, we also energetically wished the same for the entire planet. We know "entire planet" is a lot to undertake, but once you feel that compassion is present in yourself and your closest relationships, you engage the principle that a rising tide lifts all boats. People like the Dalai Lama anchor the quality of compassion on the planet so that others can emulate their nature. Imagine if compassion disappeared entirely from the planet. What a disaster that would be! Compassion is essential for our survival, and the Dalai Lama can't do it by himself. One of the best ways to help yourself and others is to move through the world with compassion.

A lot has been written about compassion. Here is a blog entry that we liked from Penny Lee, freelance writer and blogger:

> Life is about choices. That is because there is no other greater truth. One of your most important choices is choosing compassion over judgement, compassion over violence, compassion over indifference. Without knowing or showing compassion you will not know real love. Compassion comes from the heart, the emotional center of your being. To be able to show compassion you much first have it for yourself. You must love yourself before you can love someone else. You need to show kindness and understanding to yourself so you can show it to others. Cut yourself a little slack!

Seeking External Validation

Kent was well into his thirties before he began to understand that feeling good about himself was not going to come from what he did, what he owned, or who he knew. Nothing external—circumstances, people, or events—was going to make him comfortable in his own skin. He was going to have to be his own source of unconditional love.

Kent grew up on the modest side of the tracks in the 1940s in Libertyville, Illinois, and was twelve years old before he realized there were people who had a lot more money than his family. He was invited to a birthday party by a girl whose father was a doctor. They lived on the fancy side of the tracks, a part of town Kent had literally never seen before. It was a real eye-opener to him, his first realization that some people lived more luxuriously than he did.

A year later, Kent's family moved to a fancier suburb to gain access to a better school district. This only reinforced his perception that there were those who had a lot more than his family—more status, more money, more sophistication. College was more of the same, and by then, he was intent on being included in the group that had the "more," regardless of his modest background. So the pretending became even more intense. That included having less contact with his parents, because in his mind, they were evidence that he was a nobody socially!

Starting his business career after college reinforced for him that who you know was important. His employer, an advertising agency, suggested he join the exclusive downtown University Club so he could meet movers and shakers from the business community (potential ad clients).

Marilyn grew up under different circumstances. Her father was a college-educated mechanical engineer and celebrated inventor. She had the status Kent sought. Kent was convinced he was marrying up when he married Marilyn. Although she came from a "good" family, hers was also a liberal family (born and raised in San Francisco). Right after the marriage, Marilyn questioned Kent's membership in the University Club, because they did not accept Jews. She reminded him that their best friends at the time were Jewish. Kent was conflicted and felt caught between his boss's demands to make more business contacts and his wife's high moral standards and loyalty to our friends. After some consternation, Kent resigned from the club, but because he was still dependent upon other people's approval, doing so took all the courage he could muster.

Kent learned a good lesson, though. Doing the right thing is harder than doing the less courageous thing. Marilyn has continued to be his courage coach our entire life together. Kent learned to appreciate her coaching. After all, he had agreed with Marilyn that his goal was to achieve higher consciousness.

In telling this story, we're not suggesting that disconnecting from the urge to be liked is easy. It's not, and in our experience, almost everyone struggles with it. Perhaps the need for acceptance is hard-wired into our DNA, because our ancestors' basic survival was dependent upon being part of a clan. The threat of being socially ostracized was the biggest weapon the clan had to enforce conformity. We most likely still have remnants of that belief system buried deep in our genes.

Your self-worth does not come from membership in an exclusive club, your family status, or anything else external to your own inner being. Pretending to be something you're not is exhausting and ultimately unsatisfying—maybe even humiliating. It puts the focus on what you don't have, and it can definitely get in the way of making relationships workable.

CHAPTER 5

The Value of Gratitude

Life is hard. Then you die. Then they throw dirt in your face. Then
the worms eat you. Be grateful it happens in that order.
—David Gerrold

To begin this section on gratitude, we have to talk about the nature
of this universe we live in and how it operates. We suggest you
put aside your preconceived notions for a moment and consider
this: The universe is intelligent—way more than you or us. It's also
huge beyond our imaginations, yet it is personal to each of us. We
don't know why, but the universe cares for us, listens to us, and
responds to our energetic vibrations accordingly. You vibrate with
anger, sadness, resentment, or doubt and the universe responds with
more of the same in your life. The same phenomenon works for
positive emotions, such as gratitude, to which the universe responds
by giving you more to be grateful for! No kidding! That's how it
works … in our lives, at least, and we know it works in others'
lives as well. It can work in yours too. We were introduced to the
practice of ending each day by listing ten things we were grateful
for that day. Then in the morning, we began the day by expressing
our gratitude for the new day. In less than a week, more things to be

grateful for started showing up in our lives. It may sound woo-woo, but it actually worked!

All this speaks to the power of your thoughts. Bob Proctor, author of *You Were Born Rich*, says it this way: "Thoughts become things. If you see it in your mind, you will hold it in your hand." Whatever you consistently think about becomes manifest in your life. Thoughts have power. The more you put your undivided attention on your thoughts, the more your thoughts manifest what you're thinking about. It's the depth of your intention that has the power to bring into reality what you are thinking about. If you have complaints about the situations or people present in your relationship, thinking about them is crucial. If you want something to go away, stop thinking about it. Deny it the power of your thoughts. Next you might consider gratitude, which is the antidote for all anger, resentment, blame, envy—all negative emotions. Gratitude is the absence of any negative feelings, thoughts, or emotions.

If this concept is new to you, it may take some time to fully understand it. Our habitual ways of thinking and acting are so embedded in our subconscious mind that it's hard to be aware of them before they are already expressed. If it's in the subconscious, we do it on autopilot, by default. The subconscious contains decisions you made a long time ago, perhaps even as an infant, and those decisions constitute your belief system to this day.

Dr. Joe Dispenza, author, teacher, and neuroscientist, describes the power of the mind and our relationship with the Universal Mind:

> We lose 10 million cells every second and we make another 10 million cells. Something's giving us life. There is a Mind that is so much greater than our mind that has a Will so much greater than our will. And has Love for life that's so much greater than

our love for life, our personality-self. And when our will matches Its Will, when our mind matches Its Mind and when our love for life matches Its Love for us or for life, that's when It begins to respond.

First you develop a relationship with this invisible force just like you develop a relationship with your husband or your wife or your mother or father or your kids or your pets. You take time out of the day to begin to put your attention on It, begin to interact with It, and want to surrender to this Giver of life. You give this Power some pretty strong instructions and you ask for help.

We live in two states of mind: survival or creation. When we live in those states of anger or aggression or hatred or judgment or fear, anxiety or insecurity or pain or suffering or depression over time, the brains creates chemicals that activate a stressful states of mind. It's the redundancy of the chemicals that push the genetic buttons that begin to cause chronic disease.

You see, every time we have a thought we make a chemical. So if we have a great thought or, if we have an unlimited thought, we make chemicals that make us feel great or feel unlimited. If we have negative thoughts or self- depreciating thoughts, we make chemicals that make us feel negative or unworthy. So this immaterial thing called thought fires a set of circuits in the brain that produces a chemical to signal the body for us to feel exactly the way we're just thinking.

The moment we feel the way we think, we begin to think the way we feel, which produces more chemicals for us to think (This creates a big loop.) the way we feel. And this loop, the cycle of thinking and feeling, and feeling and thinking creates what I call a state of being and it's the cycle of thinking and feeling, and feeling and thinking over time that begins to condition the body to memorize that emotional state better than the conscious mind.

We owe a great deal of gratitude to Dr. Dispenza. After a lot of study, we have come to understand that his neurologically based teaching is, in essence, the same teaching of the great spiritual masters, such as Jesus, Buddha, and Gandhi. Truth is truth both scientifically and spiritually.

Living Life from Your Essence Consciousness

Imagine you are two energy fields or centers: The first center we'll call the witness consciousness, pure awareness, the silent observer, the higher self, or your essence. The second energy center is the field of personality, circumstances, beliefs, and experiences. Let's call this field the neurotic self (an expression borrowed from Michael Singer, author of *The Untethered Soul*).

Many people live their lives in the second field, often not even aware that they have a higher field of consciousness. Even those of us who know that the higher field exists can get caught up in our neurotic tendencies and not know how to extract ourselves.

Our neurotic tendencies constantly demand attention, distracting and disempowering the higher self to the point where the we forget that we have a choice to ignore or rise above this neurotic behavior. The movement from pure awareness to dysfunctional behavior occurs so fast that we can lose sight of the fact that there is a moment of choice—a choice to stay on the higher ground. There's a good chance that denying our neurotic demands will bring up feelings of pain and fear—two things we are trying desperately to avoid. The neurotic self knows this and uses it to continue to distract our higher selves from claiming their rightful positions as our essence selves. So we go through life complying with the neurotic self's demands rather than facing and conquering the blocked negative emotions that are stored deep within the subconscious. But there is hope—*big hope.*

We invite you to make a commitment to self-investigation with the promise that this will lead to self-mastery (liberation!). Start to pay very close attention to yourself—your feelings, responses, opinions, and beliefs—as often as possible in the beginning and then eventually every moment (Eckhart Tolle calls this the "Now Moment"). See where the neurotic self makes demands to be heard, to be in charge, to state its opinion regardless of the outcome. When you see the neurotic self raising its demanding head, stop it in its tracks. This is the moment of choice you previously did not know you had. Observe it without complaining about it. What you resist persists! Stay in the higher consciousness and just witness the neurotic self trying to run your life without permitting the higher self to have a say in things. Yes, you do have that power!

When you begin to claim this power, there will most likely be fear or pain. Feel it. Be vulnerable to it. Tell yourself that this one experience of pain or fear is far better than a lifetime of being enslaved by fear and pain. See this moment as a gift from the universe, not an experience to be avoided at all cost. Know that what is being asked is that you develop the necessary qualities to overcome the pain, qualities you have not previously used but that are resident in your higher self. Once this occurs, you will be a more enlightened, awake, and aware individual than you were before. You will have attained a degree of self-mastery that feels so good, you will wonder why you haven't done it before.

Know that you now have the strength, courage, and wisdom to repeat this process until all your stored negative emotional blocks have been cleared and your neurotic self has been put to rest for good! For more information on this process, we recommend you read Dr. Joe Dispenza's book, *How to Break the Habit of Being Yourself*. Referring back to the discussion on cognitive dissonance, the title of this book is a perfect example. It certainly got our attention.

Curiosity Is a Unique Human Quality

Curiosity may be the most important ingredient in the human survival drive. If curiosity weren't one of our most basic drives, we would all still be living in caves and hunting with bows and arrows. On the other hand, social mores tell us that curiosity killed the cat. Maybe curiosity pointed in the wrong direction becomes nosy and gossipy, but when applied properly, curiosity can lead to self-mastery, as well as collective advancement (which is why we don't still live in caves).

Yet, in our counseling experience, we see lots of couples who ask the same question over and over again: "Why can't my partner behave the way I want him/her to?" Why indeed? Because it's the wrong question. A better question might be, "Why can't I accept the behavior of my partner just the way it is, even though it differs from mine?" Isn't it curious that most of us want to make everything outside of ourselves the same as us? Why is that? Experts would tell us that in order to survive, our ancestors had to develop a healthy suspicion of strangers. Since the time of the earliest homo sapiens, there has been an aversion to differences. Maybe that was for good reason back then, but today it's not working—in marriages or in global relationships. Our only enemy is our own ignorance.

Ignorance is what makes marriage hard work! And the cure to ignorance is curiosity—curiosity about what makes us tick and why it's okay, and even essential, that I tick and you tock. Tick must celebrate, adore, and welcome everything about Tock, and vice versa. If Tick could successfully turn Tock into Tick, then life would be only *tick, tick, tick, tick*, instead of *tick-tock, tick-tock, tick-tock*. How dull would that be? And yet when we wish our partners would behave the way we want them to, we are in effect, trying to eliminate all tocking in our lives.

The appropriate question to ask is, "Why do I want to eliminate all tocking from my life?" Because an aversion to anything "strange" in our lives is buried deep in our genetic coding. Okay, fair enough. Maybe that is the default position in your DNA, but that doesn't mean it's serving you in your marriage relationship (or any other relationships). That brings us back to curiosity, this time as it relates to how we can change our primordial DNA coding. That seems like a huge barrier to overcome just to have a workable marriage relationship!

Maybe not. Scientists are now discovering that our DNA, rather than being fixed in time, is actually monitoring signals from the environment all the time and responding accordingly. You actually can change your genetic coding by sending different signals to your DNA. What kind of signals? you might ask. Knowing that our DNA responds to our environments and that in this case we're trying to change our genetic coding about strangers, the new signals would be acceptance, love, peace, compassion, and other similar qualities. Does watching the ten o'clock news send love, peace, and compassion signals to your DNA? Probably not. Then stop watching the ten o'clock news. Does holding a grudge against someone send signals of love, peace, and compassion to your DNA? No? Then stop holding grudges. How about getting upset with congested traffic on the freeway? The nature of the environment determines the nature of the signals you're sending to your DNA. If you want DNA coding that is not threatened by strangers and unfamiliar or unwanted situations, then perhaps you need to rethink (that is, be curious) about what environments will change the signals being sent to your DNA.

Curiosity leads to familiarity and understanding. Sometimes questions are more important than answers—focus on the what, not the why or the how. It's time to realize that Universal Intelligence is in charge, and it has a plan and a way that far exceeds your ability to run your own life

Life is a fast-flowing river of change, yet humans often act as if it isn't so. They stick with the status quo, stay in the comfort zones, and play it safe. *Don't confuse people with the facts; their minds' are made up.* We recommend you stay open at the top, try new things, change your mind from time to time, and be a life-long student. Kent was a registered Republican when we met. He had even been president of the Young Republicans Club in college. His parents were also Republicans. Marilyn was a Democrat from a liberal San Francisco family. Within a few years, Kent changed his registration to Democratic—no fuss, no fights, no intense debates. It just happened. Shift happens!

Celebrate Your Uniquenesses

Kent loves and adores about 90 percent of Marilyn and would not change a thing about it. The other 10 percent, not so much. Well guess what? That's Kent's tough luck, because that 10 percent isn't going to change just because he doesn't care for it so much. And besides, he can take to heart his own advice: be grateful—grateful that it's 90/10 and not 40/60. Besides, that 10 percent is there for a divine reason; it is Kent's teacher. The principle is, what you object to is your growing edge; there are lessons for him to learn and new qualities for him to acquire as he investigates why that 10 percent irritates him. Chances are, there are qualities in himself that he doesn't want to admit to, so rather than resolving them himself, he projects them onto Marilyn and calls it her fault. Hmm, what if that's a universal principle that is true for all of us, that what we don't like in another is an unattractive aspect of ourselves that we keep buried deep inside? Carl Jung said it this way: "Knowing your own darkness is the best method for dealing with the darknesses of other people." Jung also said, "We cannot change anything unless we first accept it."

Here are some aspects of our relationship that have been keys to our happiness:

- We are equally strong, opinionated, and willful, but we make it a dance, not a conflict.
- We let any conflict (also called contrast) create clarity, not conflict.
- The balance of power between us is equal; there is no victim or victor.
- We don't keep score.
- We share the leadership of our relationship.
- We are both high energy and enjoy being on the go.
- We are both optimistic and have faith that all is well and all will be well.

Conflict Is Just Unrealized Coherence/Cooperation

Life is full of contrast, and contrast can either lead to conflict or clarity. Most people don't like conflict, not realizing that it is a gift from God to help us develop the new qualities necessary to overcome, resolve, or transcend the conflict. This means learning to live without objecting to anything that is occurring in your life. All objection is an expression of unhappiness. If you want to be happy, stop objecting. It's that simple.

Embrace change, because that's all there is. Life is constantly changing. To resist change is to tell God you don't like the way He/She/It is running the universe.

We have found in our relationship that our similarities are easy to live with; it's our differences that help us find common ground (another way of saying that we are moving from *you* and *me* to *we*). Let your differences be the things that fascinate you most about each other. There is no right and wrong, just seven billion different ways of expressing human life on this planet.

Conflict in your relationships can be healthy. We still have conflicts in ours. Conflict is anything that moves you out of your comfort (safety) zone. We all have one, and it's not very wide. Your comfort zone is the fortress you have built around yourself to keep from feeling the pain of those things you consider uncomfortable. Committed couples are going to push each other's discomfort buttons, but this doesn't have to create create a World War in your relationship. What we do is tell ourselves that these default responses are old habits and survival mechanisms that we still have stored in our reptilian brains. They come out once in a while to play. We just step back until they wear themselves out, and then we go back to a position of mutual love and respect.

The Buddhists have the right idea about conflict. Just observe it. Resisting it or expressing it gives the conflict more power. Just put the light of your observation on it. Conflict is a form of darkness, and the one thing darkness doesn't like is light. It's the same for fear, resentment, and all our other lower emotions. Light, like love, is a universal solvent or antidote.

CHAPTER 6

Discovering That *We* Is One

Relationships are all there is. Everything in the
universe only exists because it is in relationship
to everything else. Nothing exists in isolation.
We have to stop pretending we are individuals that can go it alone.
—from *Never Eat Alone* by Margaret J. Wheatley

Kent is who he is because of his life with Marilyn and vice versa. We complete each other. We can tell you that being *we* is more fun than being *me*. We are so grateful to have discovered this. It's not all about *me* anymore. The highest spiritual practice is to surrender our free will back to God, saying "I would rather do Your will than mine." Infinite joy outweighs finite happiness anytime. So a committed relationship is a laboratory where we can practice the art of "nullifying our something-ness," making us willing to surrender our privilege of individual choice to the One (and to the *we* in our relationship).

Ask yourself how you are different because of a significant other in your life—or your boss, sibling, parent, or friend. Who would you be if these people had not come into your life? Are there any qualities or attributes you have had to develop in order to stay in relationship with them? Patience? Assertiveness? Charity? Understanding? Everything in life is in relationship with everything else, and in order to make the dance of life work, our natures all ebb and flow.

Actually, giving up your frame of reference is enlightened self-interest. Doing what's right for the relationship is the more elegant choice. This is what's needed right now on the macro level of civilization. Putting our own self-interests first is counter-productive to the scientific and spiritual truth that we are all one on one Earth, dependent upon each other and on one Life Source.

As we mentioned earlier, years ago it dawned on us that we would rather be with each other than with anyone else. That's when we knew the *we* had taken hold. We learned the highest spiritual teaching is "we are one"—one with all that is, which we can call God, Universal Intelligence, One Consciousness, Source, Allah, or Love. The best way to have a deep experience of this oneness is with a committed life partner. If we can't be one with each other, how can we be one with God?

Here's a fun thing to try in your relationship: Make a list of the qualities you now manifest as a result of your life with your partner. Share those lists with each other. Follow with a ceremony or celebration to consecrate what you have each become.

Dropping Our Religious Identities

We were both raised Protestant Christians. We were married in an Episcopal church in Kansas City and established a membership in an Episcopal church in Pacific Palisades when we moved to California. But it wasn't long before our study of *Jesus as Teacher* (the great example, not the great exception) led us to rethink our religious affiliation. Critical study of the New Testament led by Prof. Harry

Rathbun of Stanford and supported by writings of Christian biblical scholars made our transition easy. Rather than being a rejection of the traditional Christian Jesus who sat at the right hand of God, we found a more enlightened and relatable Jesus who walked the earth just as we are now and had some personal experiences that are still relevant to our lives today.

Without the Christian structure and dogma, we were on our own to re-create our own spiritual beliefs, replacing those that we had been born into and accepted by default. Here's another piece of advice: don't believe everything your mind thinks, because it was "programmed" by others at an age before you had your own power of discernment. This is an important issue to get straight in your own head. Do you live in a friendly universe, as Albert Einstein believed, or do you think you need to build defense mechanisms (i.e., personalities, egos, images) to survive, as you were most likely taught by your parental figures?

Virtually every human being is defensive. Unfortunately, as very young children we were taught that the world can be unsafe and that we needed to prepare ourselves by creating a defense mechanism to guard against anything painful or unpleasant. "Hot buttons" were installed that act as signals to alert us when someone or something is getting through our defenses. Think of it as going through life wearing a suit of armor. The minute you try to relate with another person, it's as if you both are wearing suits of armor and yet are trying to be gracefully in synch. It's awkward at best, often messy. Defense systems are not 100 percent bullet proof. Hot buttons do get pushed.

We were blessed. We pushed very few of each other's hot buttons in the early years of our marriage. When it finally got serious, we had some psychological tools at our disposal, one being the "projection" theories of Carl Jung mentioned earlier. We could also add Ralph

Waldo Emerson who said, "People seem not to see that their opinion of the world is also a confession of character."

We got it! Even though we pushed each other's hot buttons, we didn't install them, therefore we were not responsible for the reaction they caused. If one of Kent's buttons goes off, it's his problem, not Marilyn's. One hundred percent of the time. End of story! No matter how mad you are, or how sure you are that the other person is to blame, it's your problem—pure and simple. And you can resolve it without involving the other person.

Our religious metamorphosis was from accepting an external Christian belief system (Jesus and God are in the distant heavens) to having our own internally defined spiritual belief system (where God/Source can be tapped into). When this all happened—about a dozen years into our marriage—it proved to be an ideal time for us to redefine what our marriage relationship meant to us and what our vision was for our marriage: forever just married. Today, when Marilyn conducts a wedding ceremony, she makes a big point of this, but it took us a while to clarify why we were married.

Consider this: we are spiritual beings having a human experience. Or, said another way, we are eternal souls that have finite bodies to navigate through the life of form on this planet at this time. Stick with us, here. We know this is a little heady but …

There seems to be pretty general agreement among all humans that we live in a uni-verse—that it is *one*—and that all things are interrelated and interconnected. Everything is an expression of the One. Chief Seattle said it this way: "Humankind has not woven the web of life. We are but one thread within it. Whatever we do to the web, we do to ourselves. All things are bound together. All things connect."

You Are Not Damaged Merchandise

Despite what you've been told, you are never wrong, worthless, less-than, or any other negative statement people have made about you—or that you have made about yourself. Do you make mistakes? Yes, but because society has such a negative interpretation of the word *mistake*, we prefer to say that you've "missed the mark." We are all still in process—still learning—and we will continue to miss the mark sometimes. When a youngster sits down at the piano to become a master pianist, the teacher doesn't call every misplayed note a mistake. It is the learning process. You only know that you have hit the mark when you sometimes miss it. That's the nature of living in a dualistic reality.

And since this is true of you, it is also true of everyone else. They're not broken either, just missing the mark as they grow along the way. What would life be like if you always thought of other people's misfires as just missing the mark, not making an error or being insufficient. There would be no need for judgment—discernment, yes, but not full out criticism and calling people wrong. If we could all believe this way, the world would be a mighty different place.

This was a big lesson for Kent to learn. His parents modeled more judgmental behavior than Marilyn's, and thus he often found himself in the early years of marriage perceiving aspects of Marilyn as insufficient, "requiring" him to fix her. There is a kind and gentle way to give each other feedback, but it must be delivered with no attachment or expectation that the other will agree with your reflection. This is a delicate dance, and a great deal of compassion is required. Even though Kent often did not realize it, the "feedback" he was giving Marilyn was really just "projection" of his own shadow-side onto Marilyn. If we can realize that we're all one in our human frailties as well as our godliness, it makes it easier to accept the shortcomings we see in others, because we are all works in progress.

It is far better to love and have compassion in order to smooth out the rough spots in a relationship than to object and wish the other were more like you.

The Power of *No*

Many personality profiling systems postulate that our coping mechanisms are learned at a very early age. Based on early experiences that suggest the world is an uncongenial place, infants unconsciously make choices that determine how they will ensure their own survival. The condensed articles in this section suggest that the predominate admonition children hear from their parents is *no*. Based on this, it's not too hard to understand why people have trouble manifesting the good that they seek in their lives—negative childhood conditioning is deeply embedded in their belief systems. Giving up these beliefs feels like we are making ourselves vulnerable and unsafe—the same feelings we had as children and have been trying to avoid ever since. But in fact, just the opposite is true.

We believe God's abundance is unlimited and unconditional. All that is required is for us to give up all thoughts of *no*. Imagine what our lives would be like if as children we were taught the following:

- You can have whatever you want.
- You can have it right away.
- You can have as much as you want—forever.
- You don't have to pass a test to get it.
- Getting it is not conditional upon being "good."
- There's no outer authority you have to please to get it.
- There's more than enough for everybody.
- You don't have to compete with others to get it.
- There's no effort involved; just say yes to the good you desire.

It's never too late to rethink early survival choices that seemed to work then but are not working now. Through self-examination, we can identify the unproductive beliefs deep in our unconscious minds that are keeping us from our good. Then we can systematically make new decisions about each of those misbeliefs, replacing them with the understanding that it is our birthright to have complete, total, and unconditional abundance—physical, mental, emotional, and spiritual.

What Others Say about the Power of No

Desi Williamson writes the following in his book *Get Off Your Assets!: How to Unleash the Power in You,*

> If it's true that we have the power to choose how we feel, why do most people choose the negative? It's because WE'RE BORN TO WIN, BUT PROGRAMMED TO FAIL! We are programmed into the negative from the moment we come into this world. It starts with our upbringing. By the time you reach the age of 18, you've heard the word 'no' 200,000 times, seen 30,000 acts of violence, and have received more than 12 million messages in the form of advertising telling you how to look, what to eat, and how to feel. No wonder most of us grow up with a negative self-image.

Is your life tied up in "nots"? All *not* thoughts give energy to what you don't want. It's better to think about what is possible or what you do want. Saying or thinking *not* is just another way of saying *no*. This includes saying things like the following:

not a chance
not a good fit
not a good idea
not able
not about to
not acceptable
not agreeable
not appreciated
not appropriate
not approved
not available
not before you (eat, do your homework, wash your hands, etc.)
not believable
not conceivable
not convinced
not cool
not done
not enough
not even
not exactly
not fair
not funny
not getting it
not going my way
not going to happen
not good enough
not happy about it
not if I have to _____ (fill in the blank)

not if I have anything to say about it
not if it costs money
not in my backyard
not in my lifetime
not in the foreseeable future
not interested
not like me
not listening
not loved
not lucky
not me
not much
not my job
not my style
not nice
not now
not on my watch
not open
not permitted
not pleased
not possible
not prepared
not pretty
not qualified
not quite
not ready
not really
not right
not safe
not simple

not smart

not so fast

not sure

not tasty

not the right fit

not the right time

not thinkable

not time

not today

not trained

not trustworthy

not unless you (apologize, give
me a kiss, save the money, etc.)

not until

not what I want

not while I'm in charge

not willing

not without me

not working

not worthy

not yet

There are several other studies on the effects of *no* on young people.

Nina Spencer, "It's Only Words?," www.ninaspencer.com:

> A UCLA survey from a few years ago reported that
> the average one-year-old child hears the word, No!,
> more than 400 times a day! You may, at first, think
> this must be an exaggeration but consider this ...
> when we tell a toddler No! we usually say, No, no,
> no! That's three times in three seconds! If that child
> is particularly active, perhaps it's true ... perhaps
> that child really does hear NO mega times a day.
> And, although it's a good thing that they come
> to understand NO early (so that they can live to
> celebrate a second birthday!), the bottom line is
> that toddlers, from all cultures and across all time
> lines, learn what to do by constantly being told
> what not to do. Then they grow up. They go to
> work ... and the pattern of speaking and learning
> is set from the earliest of days. So, by the time they

hit the workforce, even if they are very positive, energetic and optimistically focused individuals, they are probably speaking with negative language throughout each and every day without even knowing it! It's always more powerful, influential and persuasive to say what you do want rather than what you don't want.

Happy Child: Negative Statements:

Do you realize that the brain cannot process a negative command or statement? If you say to your child "be careful, don't spill your milk" as they carry the glass full of milk across the kitchen, the child has to actually think of spilling the milk so that it can take the necessary action not to do it. We tend to get what we focus on and so by the child thinking of spilling milk that is often what tends to happen which normally results in a loud "But I told you not to spill that milk." So the moral of the story is ask for what you want, not what you don't want.

Australian Association for Research in Education: The Relationship between Significant Others' Positive and Negative Statements and Self-Talk, Self-Concepts and Self-Esteem:

Studies which have investigated the relationships between statements made by significant others and self-perceptions have found that positive interactions and statements made by significant others were related to high self-esteem and that negative interactions were associated with low self-esteem.

Additionally, statements by significant others have also been found to be related to children's self-talk. Further, a number of studies have reported associations between self-talk and self-perceptions. Collectively the results of these studies suggest that self-talk may play a mediating role between statements made by significant others and self-concepts and self-esteem.

There is evidence that indicates that verbal abuse (negative statements by significant others) adversely affects self-esteem and self-concept. […] Joubert (1991) investigated self-esteem and mother and father treatment of self when younger and found that men with high self-esteem tended to have fair mothers, who were interested in their activities and less likely to engage in verbal abuse, whilst high self-esteem in women correlated with parental praise, interest, and less verbal put-downs.

Positive statements correlated positively with self-esteem and non-academic self-concepts, while negative statements correlated negatively with reading self-concept and with relations with mother and father self-concepts. Interestingly, positive statements were more highly related to self-esteem suggesting that their presence or absence appeared to have a stronger influence on self-esteem when compared to negative statements.

Embrace Change

Change is a big subject—as big as the universe, actually. Everything in the universe is in motion—changing—all the time. We call it evolution. The truth is, life is a verb, not a noun. Nouns can stand still; verbs cannot. They are always becoming. Yet humans seem to want everything to stay in place so they can have the illusion of being in control, deciding what will come into their lives and what won't. This is called the comfort zone. Actually, it's the "discomfort zone," because it is what causes us pain and suffering. We hold on to that which evolution is trying to remove from us, and by holding on, we are resisting the entire force of evolution. Ouch! That's got to cause pain and suffering.

Some change we like (being promoted at work), and some we don't (having our property taxes increased). The reason for this is that we have preferences and desires based on our early childhood training by the authority figures around us. These preferences are so deeply embedded in us that we seldom bring them to our frontal cortex consciousness. The hard fact is, these preferences are often not based on our highest self-interest. Think sugar, for instance, or hating to exercise. Dr. Michael Bernard Beckwith of Agape International Spiritual Center calls these preferences "coagulated thought forms" that distort our vision. The ideal state of mind is clear of any likes or dislikes. It is neutral to all. We know it's hard to believe, but life is happier and more fun if you remain in a state of equilibrium. Instead of settling for temporary happiness and suffering in world of desire and preferences, choosing a world of equilibrium produces a higher state of contentment and satisfaction.

We like to think of the universe as a dance partner, and it is always taking the first step. It's our task to recognize that step and act accordingly, in a way that moves gracefully with this dance partner rather than stepping on toes. When it comes to committed relationships, what this means is that you have to stop objecting to what has already happened. The universe (through your partner or spouse) took the first step already, and now it's your move. You have the choice to move gracefully or to resist moving at all. If you're in a state of equilibrium, the next move is easy. If you're still stuck in the attitude of automatic response, your move is most likely going to be a reflection of your unconscious belief system. Your mission, should you decide to take it, is to become more familiar with your BS (belief system) and to decommission it in favor of higher more elegant choices that are more beneficial to you, your partner, and the world. That's not an easy job, of course, but elsewhere in this book you'll find some good advice on how to accomplish the job.

For years, our relationship was driven by our unconscious belief systems, which created lots of pain and suffering. Gradually, through the study of modern psychology and spiritual teachers, we gained both an intellectual and spiritual understanding of how to let our guards down and become vulnerable and authentic.

Have a Plan Based on a Purpose

Chances are, you've never heard of a couple who has written a game plan or standard operating system for their marriage. If you and your partner were to have a deep discussion about marriage, you'd probably uncover some disagreements or opposing expectations about what marriage is and is not. Rather than leave these disagreements buried deep in your belief systems to rear their ugly head sometime in the future, why not deal with them when you're both unemotionally rational?

And while you're at it, include a list of each other's strongest characteristics, too, so when conflict does arise, you can refer back to this list and perhaps have some compassion for the other, rather than just objecting. The results of our discussions are shown in the following charts.

Kent is …	Marilyn is …
• head based	• heart and head based
• task oriented first	• relationship oriented first
• impatient, restless	• patient, calm
• a generalist	• good with details
• big picture oriented	• likes all the facts
• high energy	• high energy
• intellectually curious	• intellectually curious
• likes people	• likes people
• initiating	• initiating and discerning
• function first, then form	• form and function together
• strong willed	• strong willed but with discernment
• rush forward	• slow and steady wins

You Do Not Need Each Other to Be Whole

Very often, couples have deep expectations that their partners are supposed to complete them. We do gravitate to mates who have the qualities we think we lack, but that doesn't mean our mates can fix the areas of ourselves we think are incomplete. It just means that our mates can be our models and mentors to help us self-correct our weaker tendencies. A marriage relationship is actually a real-time laboratory where you can be vulnerable and open to growing and changing with the support of your partner.

Here's our list of what marriage is and is not:

Committed Relationship is <u>not</u>	Committed Relationship is
• for economic stability • for sex • for having kids • for companionship • for social status • for conforming to societal norms • for helping you feel good about yourself	• for teaching, supporting, and celebrating each other • for giving each other honest reflection • for learning relationship skills • for advancing your spiritual path to higher consciousness • for experiencing the joys and sorrows together

Ultimately, here's what works and doesn't work in our relationship:

Works	Doesn't Work
• never forgetting the *love* that first brought us to together and how good it felt then and *now* • agreeing to a plan for our marriage that we can both buy into unequivocally • never going to bed with a fight, argument, or disagreement unresolved • knowing that marriage is a real-life laboratory for coaching and inspiring each other to higher consciousness	• keeping score • holding grudges • taking things personally • trying to change the other • refusing to change • living in the past • playing too small • staying in our comfort zones • wanting to be in control

It's Not Our Job to Fix Each Other,
but We Are Each Other's Teachers

We have often asked ourselves what we saw in each other, given that we fell in love so quickly. Kent definitely felt he was getting a woman who would reflect well on him and lift his social status, but that was a secondary feeling, not the primary cause for his unconditional love of Marilyn. Marilyn thought Kent was fun and playful and would be an adventuresome person to spend time with. Neither of us thought, *Oh, thank God. With this person as my life partner, I will now feel complete, whole, and adored, free of that subtle feeling that I'm not good enough.* We already liked ourselves just fine, thank you. Maybe even a little too much. We both definitely had reasonably well-adjusted self-esteems.

We didn't think ourselves into love. We just fell! Let go. Surrendered to the overwhelming feeling of passion. We remember another couple, friends of ours, who were also trying to decide if they should get married. They kept asking us, "how do you know for sure that you love each other enough to get married?" Obviously, falling in love for them was at least partly a mental decision. They did finally get married and sadly divorced twenty years later. As we look back on it, we can see that they both brought needs into the marriage. He had an alcoholic father growing up, and she was bipolar, which got worse when kids came on the scene. The unspoken expectation was that these sad childhood stories would be healed in the marriage. But without a strong common agreement on the purpose for their marriage, it unraveled instead.

There is no judgment intended here. We certainly can't know all of what went on in their relationship, but when we counsel couples today, we sometimes see similar challenges due to a lack of understanding of the deepest purpose of the couple-ship. What happens is both partners have some hole or wound from their past that they are expecting their partner to fill or heal.

You can see how this might happen. Virtually everyone is raised by parents who send a very strong message to their child or children: "It's your job to make me happy. When your behavior makes me happy, I'm happy. When I'm cranky, it's your fault." Wow, that's a heavy burden for small children to carry, yet we do try. And this pattern continues when we are adults; we look outside ourselves to people, events, and circumstances to validate us and make us happy. So guess what? This same dynamic shows up in marriage relationships. "It's your job to make me happy, to love me more than I love myself, so that the hole or wound I feel will go away."

While healing is a do-it-yourself task, deep compassion in a relationship can stimulate a healing process in both partners. The lyrics of a song often sung by Dr. Rickie Byars Beckwith, musical director of the Agape International Spiritual Center, say it all:

> I love myself so much,
> So I can love you so much,
> So you can love you so much,
> So you can start loving me.

Anthony Robbins, motivational coach, says it this way:

> Some of the biggest challenges in relationships come from the fact that most people enter a relationship in order to get something. They're trying to find someone who's going to make them feel good. In reality, the only way a relationship will last is if you see your relationship as a place that you go to give, and not a place that you go to take.

Your partner can't do something for you that you can't do for yourself, such as love you unconditionally. Self-esteem comes from within, not from any external validation, such as from your partner, boss, friend, or parent. Remember what Sally Kempton, Manhattan socialite-cum-swami, said, "Self-love suppressed becomes self-loathing."

Thanks to a lifetime of spiritual study, what we've come to believe is that we are already whole and perfect and require no "fixing." Dr. Gail Brenner, a licensed psychologist, has written a book entitled *The End of Self-Help* in which she rejects the notion that we need help because we are wounded or broken. On the contrary, in the spiritual realm, we are whole, perfect, and complete. That which created us loves us unconditionally just the way we are. We're not saying you have to believe in some god (which is after all undefinable), but we are asking you to believe in life, which shows up perfectly in everything it creates.

We understand you may not totally buy into this concept of perfection right away. We didn't either for many years. In fact, we've found most people are afflicted with the illusion that they are wounded and suffering from not being adequately loved, starting with their parents who were inadequate in some or many ways. Take a moment to ponder this: somewhere in your belief system, you hold on to the thought that the parenting you received fell short of your needs and wants, and you are still looking for someone or something that will fix that condition for you.

If you resonate with this statement, you have some forgiving to do (more about this elsewhere in this book). You also have some major expectations to drop if your committed relationship is going to thrive.

A common admonition of many human potential workshops, books, CDs, and more is, "When are you going to drop your childhood emotional baggage and move on with your life?" Instead, some say, "That's my story, and I'm sticking to it." There's a tale about a wise tribal shaman who got tired of people complaining that their lives were worse than everybody else's in the village. So the shaman arranged for everyone to put his or her "life" in a bag and place it in the middle of the village square, with the understanding that each could take someone else's bag and make it his or her own. Of course, you know what happened. After much hemming and hawing, each person took back his or her own bag.

So, what's the lesson in this old folk tale? Bloom where you're planted. Play the hand you were dealt. Ride out on the horse you came in on. Drop your old luggage and move on ... or pick up your bag of human limitations and work with it? Which is it?

In our experience, the best way to deal with the weight of "your story" is not to take it too seriously. The Enneagram personality profiling system has helped us immensely in this regard. It turns out our stories are not who we are. They're where we hide out. They're our defense mechanisms, our safety zones, the camouflage or suit of armor we wear to protect ourselves from what we believe is an unfriendly world.

Our stories aren't even that unique. Many profile profiling systems indicate that all human behavior falls into archetypical patterns that repeat over and over. Essentially, every nth person in the world behaves very similarly to the way you do. That's humbling—and liberating, because it allows us to look objectively at our stories and who we think we are and recognize them as a collection of memories, beliefs, attitudes, and responses much like that of many others.

Michael Singer, in his book *The Untethered Soul*, puts it this way:

> If you go deep enough, you can watch the psyche being built. You will see that you are in the middle of nowhere, in empty infinite space, and all of these inner objects are flowing toward you. Thoughts, feelings, and the impressions of world experiences are all pouring into your consciousness. You will clearly see that the tendency is to protect yourself from this flow by bringing it under your control. There is an overwhelmingly strong tendency to lean forward and grab onto selective impressions of people, places, and things as they flow through. You will see that if you focus on these mental images, they become part of a complex structure where there was none. You will see events that took place when you were ten years old that you're still holding onto. You will see that you're literally taking all your memories, pulling them together into an orderly fashion, and saying that's who you are. But you're not the events; you're the one who experienced the events. How can you define yourself as the things that happened to you? You were aware of your existence before they happened. You are the one who is in there doing all this, seeing all this, and experiencing all this. You do not have to cling to your experiences in the name of building yourself. This is a false self you are building inside. It is just a concept of yourself that you hide behind.

Most personality profiling systems tell us the same thing: your personality (story) is just a concept – not the real you.

Author and teacher Eckhart Tolle believes that all these experiences we're collecting are physically stored as energy inside our bodies, and because most of these experiences have some pain or trauma associated with them, Tolle calls this the "pain body." You know when someone pushes your button and you have an immediate and powerful reaction? That's your pain body being activated.

Sometimes we will trigger each other's pain body, and it will set off feelings of anger and resentment that are very unlike our normal selves. We're trapped. The pain bodies will have their way until the moment subsides. We've learned to just let this happen, viewing it as an experience separate from our higher selves. When it's over, we move on. We don't let it fester or linger. It's done; no attachment. It wasn't who we really are. We just agree that our pain bodies got activated, and now that it's over, we can resume living at our higher frequencies. We remember what the Enneagram system and Michael Singer have taught us: pain bodies are just collections of stories ("coagulated thought forms," as Michael Beckwith calls them) that reside somewhere in our deep human unconscious, unrelated to our already perfect selves.

Take a moment now and ask yourself, "Who would I be without my story?" Or another way to ask it is, "Who am I already if I remove my attachment to my story?" Yes, you can detach from your story, but it takes practice and time. Remember, we consider ourselves to be two entities: the neurotic-personality self and the higher, silent-witness self. Through self-awareness, investigation, meditation, and silent contemplation, we can begin to identify more with the silent witness and be more objective, more detached from our neurotic selves. These selves are not who we really are. They're habits, which means we've been practicing them for a long time. They're messages from our old belief systems that are stored in our subconscious brains.

Neuroscientists are telling us that the brain is not set in concrete. It's plastic and remoldable. Old habits can be changed; the pain body can be freed from unwanted behavior patterns. You do have a choice, but it requires a lot of self-observation. In time, you can actually see the habitual response rising from deep within you, creating a decision point. You can choose not to allow this habitual response to manifest. You literally make a decision to stay awake and conscious, not falling back into the habit of sleepwalking.

Impartial Self-Observation

Most people see themselves far less clearly than they think. In fact, some behavioral researchers spend their lives investigating why people understand themselves so little, often lying to themselves rather than facing the truth of themselves. According to Robert Trivers, who wrote *The Folly of Fools*,

> Deceit and self-deception are universal aspects of everyday life. There are numerous examples of deception in nature, from birds that trick other species into raising their young, to fireflies, orchids and sunfish that use sexual mimicrys and squids that camouflage themselves to hide from predators. In humans, deceit and self-deception are more complex, amusing and sometimes dangerous. We all consciously or unconsciously routinely deceive ourselves by creating or suppressing memories, rationalizing immoral behavior or boosting our own self-image.

Ultimately, Trivers believes we would live better, healthier lives by being more honest with ourselves and each other. It's one thing to knowingly tell a little white lie to your spouse, parent, boss, or whomever. It's quite a different kettle of fish to lie to yourself and then act as if you hadn't. We sometimes call it "positive thinking," "reframing," or just an innocent little rationalization. No way! We are letting ourselves off the hook, diluting ourselves, and creating a story that will require enormous amounts of energy to keep afloat.

Kent is a good example of this. While he had a relatively successful business career, he had eleven different jobs in his career. That's an average of less than three years per job. Sometimes he quit because he was unhappy with the job; other times he could tell he was not doing a good job and sensed he was going to be let go, so he quit. Only twice did he leave a job for a better opportunity. He was obviously not the hotshot adman he thought he was, but it took until the twenty-first century before he could admit that. For forty-five years, he skipped from job to job, always making a good first impression but not one that would last for the long-term. He was always a good first-impression guy, but he always lost it in the trenches. He preferred to reframe each lost job instead of doing a serious internal inventory of his strengths and weaknesses. He couldn't face the truth of himself. (Happily, in the last ten years, he has done that serious internal inventory and feels he's found his real self.)

You may not be ready to admit that you lie to yourself, but we're betting that you can remember times when you've been pretentious. We think it's the same thing as lying, sugar-coated so our egos don't have to face up to the truth of our behavior. Any way you slice it, we all do too much pretending, and it sucks!

If two people are going to develop an honest, authentic, intimate relationship that is truly unique, then you can't show up in the relationship unaware of where and how you are not being honest with yourself. Instead, we suggest you try "impartial self-observation." It's a little like pulling yourself up with your own bootstraps. If you think about it, how the hell do you do that? How can you be impartial if you're the one doing the lying? How can you observe yourself if you're the self doing the observing.

It works because there is more than one of you. There are two—the one standing in the boots and the other one doing the pulling; the one observing, and the other being observed. We realize this is probably not your everyday experience. It requires the suspension of everything you rely on to make it through life—your five senses, your rational mind, and your attachment to who you think you are (that is, your story). Where do you do this? In silence. In the space between all your doing. It's called by some the silent witness or the still point. It's the here-and-now point, not dependent upon history or the future to validate its existence.

The beautiful thing is that the silent witness is impartial yet totally understanding and compassionate. It sees the you that is lying to itself, but it doesn't judge it, reprimand it, or try to exterminate it. It just shines a light on it. It enlightens you, so to speak, and in that light, darkness or ignorance cannot exist. Once you know, you can't unknow. For some, one huge enlightened moment dispels all their internal darkness. For most of us, it's one layer of the onion at a time.

The chart below is our attempt to illustrate the process we've been discussing here. The chart represents the spectrum of human behavior, from the most corrupt on the left to the most enlightened on the right. Most of us live in the left half of the chart—moving from victim to victor but avoiding the quantum leap into the right side of the chart. As the bar in the center of the chart suggests, the price of admission to the higher levels of human behavior is facing the pain that comes when we acknowledge that we have been kidding ourselves about who and what we are.

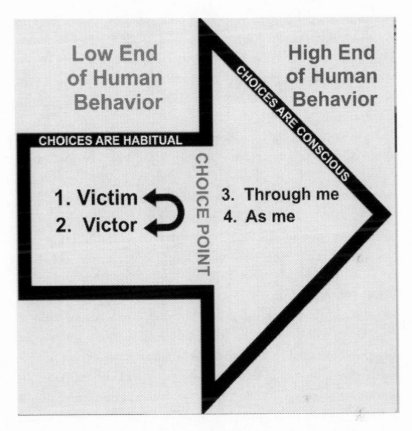

We told you this is a relationship book, but it's also all about you, because if you can be in relationship with yourself, you can be in relationship with others. And it's the avoidance of pain that is keeping you out of relationship with yourself. That painful past experience is stuffed so deep down inside you that you have almost forgotten it's there. Yet it is actively controlling your behavior every day. That pain determines your comfort zone, and if you stray too close to the edges of this zone, it reminds you the pain is still there.

If two people in relationship move out of their comfort zones at the same time, conflict occurs, often manifesting as anger, indignation, resentment, or self-justification. The point is, when this happens, you have lost track of the impartial self-observer in favor of being incredibly partial toward your own point of view. You've become defensive, because you don't want to take responsibility for finding a higher truth in the conflict. We learn this trait very early in life, because parents can place a lot of blame on their kids without even knowing it.

Can you remember a time in your childhood when your parents were scolding you for some "bad behavior" and you just fessed right up and said, "Yes, I did it." Not likely. Well, that's what we're recommending you do now as an adult: take responsibility for every criticism your internal voice throws your way, whether you think you deserve it or not. It stops conflict dead in its tracks. Force only has power when it meets resistance. It takes two to create conflict.

When you master this skill, your ability to stay in the impartial self-observer role will increase and your avoidance of painful experiences will decrease. As you continue to practice, you'll move into the "through me" section of this human behavior chart, letting Life (with a capital L) move through you without resistance or objection. You'll be present to circumstances, events, and people without objection, judgment, or opinion. You'll be neutral. You'll be in a state of equanimity. When you do this, you'll find that the behaviors you object to in others atrophy and, in the case of committed relationships, intimacy and trust appear instead.

You can print this chart in pdf format at our website (www.foreverjustmarried.com). We suggest you keep it visible during your daily routine and contemplate where you are on the spectrum as often as possible. Remember to do it impartially—no judgment or negative self-talk, just dispassionate observation.

CHAPTER 7

In It for Life

The relationship between commitment and doubt is by no means an antagonistic one. Commitment is healthiest when it's not without doubt but in spite of doubt.
—Dr. Rollo May

We are living proof of this quote. We have stayed together for fifty-plus years in spite of doubt and antagonism. Our commitment to one another is healthy because we have not denied the existence of doubt and antagonism nor have we let it destroy our marriage. We'd give in, but not up. Divorce was never an option; that was a decision we made jointly in 1973, at a spiritual retreat in northern California. It came after we had been married over a decade and had tested the tensile strength of our bonds many times. The commitment to never divorce is a little bit like training a wild horse to be bridled, saddled, and ridden. One's baser instincts don't capitulate easily. But on the other side of the struggle is a beautiful, loving relationship with amazing benefits that our wild sides could never know.

In our society, we often equate buckling under with losing. It can feel like a life sentence of imprisonment. "You're not the boss of me, buster!" is the default position of our wilder natures. And it can be triggered by the littlest things, such as "Would you put the garbage out, honey?"

Sometimes marital rifts are caused by large deal-breakers, such as infidelity. But more often than not, they're caused by the little things—not putting the cap back on the toothpaste, for instance. At least this has been true in our experience. If we examine the things in our relationship that cause antagonism, it's often the most insignificant behaviors.

Kent is a "get it done now, even if it's not perfect" kind of guy, and Marilyn is a "wait until the last moment to be sure you've thought of everything" kind of woman. For instance, when we plan a workshop together, Kent will always begin the process of developing the curriculum, hoping it will all be put to bed days before the actual event. Marilyn, on the other hand, gives her fullest and most effective attention to the curriculum in the last few days, which creates a high level of anxiety in Kent. There are lots of good reasons why Marilyn waits until later. She is waiting for her head and heart to be in agreement about the curriculum that Kent wrote from the head only. After Marilyn makes her last minute contributions to the curriculum, we always have a much better product. If she were instead to capitulate, letting Kent have his way and shutting down the development process when he wanted to, the workshop would suffer. Kent knows this, and yet the process still makes him anxious.

When other people's behaviors annoy you, it's because you have given their behavior a value. What if you said, "Their behavior is none of my business" and just moved on with your life? Moving on doesn't mean you throw them out of your life or never have anything to do with them again. It means accepting who they are and not letting it determine your own personal well-being.

Your spouse's style doesn't have to be an annoyance to you; in fact, it can be a benefit. Objecting to it is what keeps you in a state of unhappiness. Want to be happy? Don't object to anything! Yes, we know that not objecting to anything is a tall order, and we are still working on it ourselves. But we are convinced that every event is a neutral one, and it's only the value you give it that makes it positive or negative. Kent knows full well that Marilyn's approach to curriculum development (or any other project they work on together) will result in a better product, but that doesn't always prevent him from first objecting to her methods. We understand how thoroughly our habitual behaviors are hardwired in our brains, even when they are not in our best interest. We know the workable relationship advice we're giving here is not always easy to execute, but we do know for sure that it is always more deeply satisfying when we succeed in making more conscious choices instead of giving in to our baser natures.

Why do so many people seem to lack the art of relationship diplomacy? Dare we suggest that our society has become too self-indulgent? Narcissistic? Soft? Personally irresponsible? A metaphor comes to mind here about the lab test in which frogs were plunged into hot water only to jump out immediately while other frogs put intocool water that was then heated so slowly that they didn't register the change ultimately boiled to death (ugh!). Is there any chance that is what has happened to us? When our country first broke away from Great Britain, we had a common goal that superseded our individual needs to become an independent country. We would all succeed or collectively fail. Obviously, we succeeded. American culture over the last two hundred years has changed from putting *we* first to putting *me* first, and it happened so imperceptibly that we don't realize we are about to boil.

Yet, maybe we shouldn't be surprised. After all, our country was founded on the rallying cry of the Connecticut Marines in the

American Revolution: "Don't tread on me." As a nation, we have been treating the rest of the world exactly that way for over two centuries. And if you live in a collective consciousness that says "don't mess with us," that ultimately becomes your individual nature as well. Okay, so this may be a little sweeping and a lot generalized, but we think there is a point to be made here. Ask yourself, are there any places in your relationship where you make your individual survival more is more important than the survival of the relationship?

Here's an interesting thought to ponder: Is there any connection between our nation's high divorce rate and the intractable, polarized nature of the two political parties in Washington, DC? What qualities of compromise and cooperation have we lost in the last two hundred–plus years that might be needed to ensure workable relationships—both individually and collectively?

Are we sometimes polarized? Absolutely. Often, but only for a short moment. One of the reasons we named this book *Forever Just Married* is that we have divorced and remarried thousands of times, always with the same person. Every disagreement is a divorce; every resolution of conflict is a recommitment to the relationship.

Infidelity Doesn't Have to Be a Deal-Breaker

In the first ten years of our marriage, we both cheated on each other. It wasn't because we were falling out of love. Even when two people are happily married, the physical desire to copulate with a new partner still seems to reside deep in our psyches. We each wanted to have sex with another person just for the variety (at least that's what we told ourselves). This is not to imply that we didn't have a good sex life; we had a great one. Human lust is a "many-splendored thing," as the song lyric tells us. It can be a reflection of our lower, wilder natures, or it can be a consecration of two people's deep love.

Cheating transitioned to "wife swapping," which lasted about a year and involved several different couples we knew. During this time, we received a phone call from neighbors inviting us to their house for dinner, offering the vague reason that they had something to discuss with us. We assumed they wanted to wife swap, so we said yes. It turned out they wanted us to join Amway. We had a good laugh over that. Another experience we had swapping with another couple was not so laughable. After several times with them, Kent became concerned that Marilyn was becoming emotionally as well as physically involved with the other guy. This was not supposed to happen; the relationship was only to be physical. Kent broached the subject with Marilyn, and we agreed to call off the entire wife swapping adventure. We realized we were getting in over our heads, and the consequences of continuing to wife swap could have damaged or ended our relationship. We were not ready to let our marriage go down the slippery slope toward divorce. Ironically, one of the couples we swapped with did get a divorce shortly thereafter.

Let us pause here and say, we are not against divorce. Sometimes it is the appropriate decision; just not 50 percent of the time, which is the national divorce rate in our nation. Perhaps the thought of divorce is just a wake-up call that your relationship needs attention. It may be your emotional "pain body" reenacting early childhood experiences of betrayal and abandonment. The deeper the pain, the more obvious it is that you have a lot of work to do to find that internal rudder that keeps your life stable and grounded instead of easily blown over by life events. We know it worked for us. Our love for each other was so profound that even when we shared our transgressions with each other and felt the pain, we still stayed in dialogue until we found our common ground again.

Remember when we said earlier that every event in life is a neutral one and only we give it a positive or negative value? Is it possible that even infidelity is a neutral event? Ultimately, for us, it was. As we look back on our infidelities, neither of us has any emotional charge associated with those events. We have forgiven each other and have moved on.

Just for fun, Google "how to survive infidelity." Surprisingly, there are many examples. We suggest you check out the Mayo Clinic website (www.mayoclinic.org) and search the word *infidelity*.

Keeping a Secret Is the Same as Lying

Probably everyone tells little white lies. We do. There are little things we've done that we know would upset the other, so we kept them to ourselves. Actually, Marilyn believes that telling little white lies can be beneficial. It's the kind thing to do, she says. Kent doesn't know that he totally agrees, but he chalks it up to different personalities. He does know that he's more likely to offend someone than she is.

Big lies are another issue. Early in our marriage, Kent cheated on Marilyn several times while on business trips out of town, and of course, he didn't tell her. Then in the mid-1970s, we attended a spiritual retreat, and one of the exercises was to tell your spouse any transgressions you had been keeping a secret from your partner. It was an amazing experience! Kent's first emotion was absolute panic, followed by the thought, *Marilyn will kill me.* What actually happened was forgiveness on Marilyn's part and absolute relief on Kent's. *And* in the process, Marilyn admitted that she had done the same. Suddenly we realized the wisdom of the Catholic practice of confession, if done right.

We found out from this experience that it takes a lot of energy to live with secrets. At some deep level, it's emotionally draining to always have to cover up secrets. We knew it was irresponsible, and yet we were letting ourselves off the hook. That definitely was not in line with our personal goals of being authentic, transparent, and trustworthy. We were willing to make bad choices in order to maintain our images—and suffer the consequences—rather than involving each other and admitting we didn't know what we were doing. We were deluding ourselves. Some people say the most fearful thing in their lives is public speaking, and we think that's because it is closely linked to self-exposure. We don't want to reveal ourselves.

Try this exercise for yourself: Go inside and ponder the question "What is it I don't want anybody to know about me?" Dig deep. Take as much time as you need.

Now turn inside and say to your higher self,
    I have a secret that I don't want anyone to know.
    I have been this way as long as I can remember.
    The reason I don't want people to know it is _____.
    I am going to make a commitment now to reveal it to someone soon.

Write down your thoughts and decide if there is someone in your life (maybe your partner) with whom you could discuss this.

Learn from Each Other

We live in a world that encourages competition, but to win, there has to be a loser. Obviously, this kind of value system won't work in a committed relationship. Nevertheless, because we are so strongly influenced by the cultural values around us, we sometimes fall prey to it.

A committed relationship is not about keeping score or who holds the power. This is not easy, because the human animal is hardwired to survive at any cost. It's very deep in our subconscious brain to want to be in control of people and circumstances around us. If we're not in control, we're vulnerable. If we're vulnerable, we might be "killed" in whatever way we think we're in competition with everything around us.

Moving from thinking we live in an unfriendly universe to deeply knowing that the life force that activates and sustains everything is unconditionally loving is essential. You can attempt to validate this concept from a spiritual or a scientific point of view. All the world's religious and faith traditions believe that love is the universal solution to all our problems. Scientist David Bohn called it the "universal implicate order," meaning the "unbroken wholeness of the totality of existence as an undivided flowing movement without borders."

Yes, we live in a world of duality. Everything appears to be in contrast to everything else. And over the centuries, humankind has evolved belief systems around the nature of duality. Some dualities are accepted while others are rejected, and this can escalate from simple disagreements to global war. This paradigm may have worked for our ancestors, but in the nuclear age, the urge to pose as enemies can only lead to life-threatening consequences. It's time to understand the profound significance of Dr. Bohn's "unbroken wholeness of the totality of existence," and if this is true for the macrocosm, then it must also be true for us in the microcosm.

Together, we are fundamentally an unbroken wholeness. Our highest self-interest is to practice this all-is-one paradigm to the best of our abilities and to show each other where improvement is needed without the other person objecting. We help each other become more conscious, learning to break free of our conditioned behaviors and stimulating a curiosity and openness to change in ourselves and others. It means that others have qualities that we should learn to manifest in our own behavior and that we should be willing to admit that what we object to in others is buried through denial deep inside ourselves. Accepting feedback from our partners isn't easy, and chances are, the less easy it is, the more likely it is that the feedback is profoundly true and that we need to hear it. It means learning to move out of our self-centeredness and complying with the larger implicate order. In doing so, you develop a level of trust and vulnerability in the relationship that exceeds that in any other relationship in your life. Thich Nhat Hanh, the world-renowned Buddhist monk, suggests that couples who are experiencing some discomfort in their relationships and want to facilitate healing say to each other:

- Darling, I am here for you.
- Darling, I know you are there, and it makes me happy.
- Darling, I know you suffer, and I am here for you.
- Darling, I am suffering, and I need your help.
- Darling, this is a happy moment.

Learn to Live without Objecting

If it's true, which we believe it is, that life always makes the first move, then objecting to what life has just put in front of us can only cause unhappiness! It may feel good to get if off your chest, but the truth is that anytime you object, you are creating unhappiness for yourself. Objection obviously means that what you are experiencing is contrary to your belief system, otherwise you would welcome it into your life. Objecting is taking a *no* and *not me* position. What we're looking for is the *we* position and, if not a complete *yes*, at least a *maybe; I'm staying open*.

Life scares us, so we try to control it so we feel safe. That's why *no* is our default position. We learned it from our parents who objected often to our behavior and often said no to us without any good reason. In fact, we heard *no* thousands of times more than we heard *yes*. *No* is the opposite of gratitude, which is the mother of all divine qualities and the gateway to a life of abundance, happiness, and well-being.

We're not saying you should just roll over and be a doormat. That can just be another way of saying no. One thing we believe is that the universe only says yes—100 percent of the time—as it continues to roll out more and more change, more and more evolution. So if the universe only says yes, then why the heck should humans ever say no? We know we've been given free choice, but saying no to the universe is like saying you don't want the abundance, well-being, and joy that the universe is offering you without any strings attached except that you can never say no again, at least not in the spiritual sense.

Safety is an illusion. Nothing living on this planet has anything resembling the safety that many people are looking for. Life is uncertain; dance with it and enjoy it while it lasts. It will end. We live in a world of contrast. Contrast—not comfort—is our teacher, our growing edge. We have lots of contrast in our relationships, and when dealt with lovingly and creatively, the contrast turns to clarity, which makes each of us better dance partners.

You Need to Like People; They're All There Is

One way to gauge how well you like people is to ask yourself, "Do I have any pet peeves?" Take a moment and ponder this question deeply. We have never met anyone who doesn't have some pet peeves, and usually they have to do with other people's behaviors.

- "It really gripes me when thoughtless people throw litter out of their cars onto the street."
- "I hate it when drivers rush to the front of a line of cars waiting to exit the freeway and cut-in, rather than waiting in line like the rest of us."

- "Why do people always have to talk about themselves so much?"
- "Why can't emotional people get a hold of themselves and calm down?"
- "Why won't my wife ever put the cap back on the toothpaste?"
- "Only lazy people sit around drinking beer and watching football on television all day."
- "Overweight people must not have any will power."

Do any of these strike a chord? You may see them in yourself or in others. You know, of course, that many wise teachers have said that you can't see a trait in others unless you also have it in yourself. Before you say "ouch," remember that this means good as well as not-so-good traits.

We could write an entire book about where these pet peeves come from, but suffice to say, we've all got 'em, and they aren't worth having. Some people never come to this realization and spend their entire lives pushed around by their peeves. Others recognize that peeves handicap them and try to find ways to off-load them. This book is for the latter group of people.

Because we live in a world of apparent duality, which causes contrast, when we object to the contrast, pet peeves are launched. Object often enough, and deeply engrained peeves will become second nature. We don't have to become nonentities or doormats to put an end to our peeves and stop objecting to the contrast. We simply have to recognize that contrast is our friend, our blessing. Contrast is intrinsic to the infrastructure of life. Without contrast, there could be no up and down, big and small, black and white—you get the idea. We already know this, yet we continue to retain the right to object to some things, just not all things.

We give Mother Nature free passage through our minds without objecting (unless she has just delivered us three feet of snow). Why not people, as well? Perhaps the universe actually inserted contrast into our life experiences for a reason, and because of our objections, we are missing that reason. What if we saw other people's weird behaviors as potential life lessons? The phrase *no pain, no gain* comes to mind. Learning from our pet peeves may seem like no fun at first, but breaking unworkable habits is hardly ever easy. We have made it a practice, when we find ourselves angry at the behavior of another, to ask, "Where is that behavior also in us?"

As we look back over our fifty-plus years together, we can see lots of times when we objected to behaviors in one other. We can also see when we owned the objections—understanding that they were our own problems, not our partner's—and resolved them. The qualities required to make that transition turned us into more conscious people. The same thing happened when we stopped objecting to the behavior of others besides the two of us. We changed, and ironically, so did they.

Consider the possibility that the universal relationship paradigm is *no objection*. Bitching and moaning feels cathartic, but it's our observation that the universe doesn't bitch or moan or object. As Matthew 5: 45 in the New Testament tells us, "God causes the sun to rise on the evil and the good, and the rain to fall on the righteous and the unrighteous." Without objection! Since we are creations of the universe (what else could we be, after all?), our highest natures should be the same as the universe's. If the universe gives us free passage through its mind, we can learn to do likewise. It's not easy, but it is possible with concentrated mindfulness. Once you neutralize your opinions of others, it's easier to accept the other, which then leads to love for the other.

Live from a Place of Possibility, Not Reality

We live in a field of infinite possibilities, much like having access to unlimited money in an unlocked vault. The problem is, we always come out of the vault having chosen pennies and nickels instead of hundred-dollar bills. Or we think that the vault door is locked and we don't have the key.

By holding too tightly to our lives as we know them (i.e., not having the key to greater abundance), we diminish the experience of being fully alive and present—the state of being where God hangs out. So stay open to the possibility there is *more*. God's not through with you yet. Life is an adventure to be appreciated fully, not a challenge to be minimized or shut down. Go inside for a moment and ponder where you limit your experiences to those things which are congruent with your comfort zone, and then ponder where you have taken risks beyond your comfort zone and it has paid off. How does that feel? Now consider where else you might move beyond your comfort zone and find other positive new experiences. Start small and continue.

This is how life evolves—from the field of what is possible rather than what already is. This is why thinking is so powerful. Thoughts become things; first thoughts, then things. Thoughts create! Thoughts come from the field of infinite possibilities, so why not hang out in the space of possibilities all the time. Ignore current reality; it's old news (effect, not cause). Live from the place of possibility, not regret or resentment. Being grateful is the gateway to having more to be grateful for in your life. Gratitude is a self-fulfilling prophecy, but so is self-pity. It took a while in our relationship for us to feel gratitude for where we were leading each other: outside our comfort zones. At first we both resisted the new things the other was leading us into, but once we dropped our resistance, we found our lives expanded for the better. As Pema Chodron says, "It's not a terrible thing that we feel fear when faced with the unknown. It is part of being alive, something we all share."

Practicing Forgiveness

When you are learning how to forgive someone or how to forgive yourself, it is helpful to have a road map to follow. While we may think that forgiving others is something we do for them, we are actually the ones who receive the greatest benefit. How? Forgiveness sets us free as it allows us to release harbored energy, emotions, and thoughts that do not serve us.

Understanding the importance of forgiveness and its benefits can help us to better comprehend why practicing forgiveness is well worth our time. This knowledge can also provide us with the motivation we may need in order to give ourselves the gift of forgiveness. How do we know when we have some forgiving to do? When difficult emotions get triggered within us as we think about a person or situation, it's likely that we have some forgiveness work to do.

When we are feeling blocked in our lives, forgiveness can also help to clear the suppressed energy that may be weighing us down and holding us back from living the lives that we truly desire. Forgiveness work can help us to break through stagnant energy and support us in moving forward with our goals and desires.

As author and spiritual teacher Louise Hay says,

> I know that when we are stuck, it usually means there is some more forgiving to be done. When we do not flow freely with life in the present moment, it usually means we are holding on to a past moment. It can be regret, sadness, hurt, fear, or guilt, blame anger, resentment, and sometimes even the desire

for revenge. Each one of these states comes from a space of unforgiveness, a refusal to let go and come into the present moment.

Forgiveness can help you release difficult emotions and can be instrumental in helping you learn how to forgive someone (including yourself). A key element in learning how to forgive someone is to create a regular forgiveness practice. This is a great way to keep your energy up, and it will help you to stay healthy and happy. In *Chakra Clearing*, author Doreen Virtue writes, "Just as you probably wash your face every night, it's also important to cleanse your consciousness nightly so resentment won't accumulate."

Doreen recommends doing nightly releasements where you mentally review your day prior to falling asleep. Ask yourself if there is anyone from your day that you need to forgive (including yourself and even your pets, if you have them). If there is, take a few moments to do a forgiveness exercise or, if you want to keep it really simple, to say a forgiveness affirmation. A nice affirmation that Doreen recommends is, "I forgive you, and I release you. I hold no unforgiveness back. My forgiveness for you is total. I am free, and you are free." You can use this or create your own positive-affirmation statement. Saying a forgiveness affirmation may be all you do, or you could take it a step further and, after you say the affirmation, visualize and feel the forgiveness occurring inside of you. This can be very powerful!

Then, if it feels right, ask God/Spirit to assist you in making this forgiveness complete. Give thanks, allowing the sensation of gratitude to fill your heart. Then imagine sending this gratitude to the person or situation you have just forgiven.

As you become accustomed to giving forgiveness, you may even find yourself practicing forgiveness throughout the day, clearing situations as they happen or soon after when you have a few minutes to go within to forgive and release the energy of the situation.

The idea is simply to begin to incorporate the practice of forgiveness into your life on a more regular basis. Doing so will help you to experience the benefits of forgiveness on an ongoing basis.

Be Self-Curious

If you were riding the rapids in the Colorado River, how satisfied would you be if you grabbed ahold of a tree limb and tried to stay in one place. It's pretty obvious, right? The river would make your life miserable. This is a perfect metaphor for the evolutionary flow of life every moment. It seems easy to accept the fact that the river requires you to flow with it every moment, changing as necessary to navigate the rapids successfully and safely. What's not so clear is how to flow with life every moment, given that we are holding onto current beliefs and values (i.e. the limb).

Flowing with life is a big job, which we think we have made clear throughout this book. At first it's all grunt work, and it's not very rewarding. But the longer you stay with it, the more you realize that the universe's way for you is better than your own, and you'll begin to feel the peace that accompanies "not my will but Thy will be done." You don't become a God robot. You still have choices. You still run your life. But all your choices are in your own best and highest self-interest. Then if you add a committed life partner to the equation, it's pure bliss, joy, and great fun! The Bible scripture that says "make smooth the path before you" is absolutely true.

As this chapter's name implies, what's most helpful here is curiosity— not idle curiosity, but *big time curiosity*, as in your life's most passionate desire. It takes the power of curiosity and deep-seated intention to override your ego's mischievous ways of distracting you from attaining a relationship with your higher self. Curiosity can be risky. You never know what it might lead to. After all, it killed the cat (a saying that only our egos would agree with). But we really believe that curiosity is a very strong drive in human beings. Otherwise, humans would still be living in caves instead of standing on the moon.

Ask yourself what role curiosity plays in your life—not just outer curiosity about the world, but inner curiosity about you and what makes you tick. The inner journey is far more fascinating than the outer journey. Give it a try.

CHAPTER 8

Making More Elegant Choices

Right now you are one choice away from a new beginning—one that leads you toward becoming the fullest human being you can be.
—Oprah Winfrey

We observe that searching for happiness, success, and peace of mind in outer circumstances, events, and people isn't going to give us permanent peace of mind. The only real source of self-confidence is inside us—the place we're spending more and more time hanging out. Kent has stopped telling himself that his job, his partner, his car, yoga, spiritual study, and so on, are going to give him that feeling of complete satisfaction he seeks. He's getting his priorities straight. The only true source of satisfaction is the unconditional love of the life force that created us and sustains us. Since we believe the universe is one infinite field of cosmic intelligence, we must conclude that we are part of the cosmic field, not separate from it. Jesus, the master teacher, said, "The Father and I are one." Well, if he's right, then we and you are also one with the Father, however you want to define *Father*—source, creator, love, life force.

This leads us to the conclusion that what people call a "spiritual practice" is not optional. It's imperative. At this point in our lives, we think we've mastered the world of form—money, possessions, lifestyle, reputation. We've also spent a good deal of time contemplating the spiritual realm. (We have meditated every morning for over thirty years.) Even so, we wish we had connected with this wisdom earlier in our lives. Paraphrasing Jesus, if you seek spiritual wisdom first, the universe will take care of all your other needs as well. For a long time, we thought the physical world was our source. Now we know that was just an illusion. All that effort was unnecessary. All we needed to do was seek and find the spiritual wisdom that the universe is constantly expressing around and through us. Instead, we ignored it for a long time. We concede that it's not easy to let an invisible intelligence run our lives. Have you ever contemplated the possibility that there is an invisible force that is running your life and that all your efforts to be in control of your life are just getting in the way? Instead of thinking that a person or situation that you don't like should be resisted and avoided, we suggest trying to seeing that person or situation as the bearer of a gift from God that can benefit you by helping you develop a new sense of acceptance. Perhaps we could even consider that *every* person or circumstance that clashes with our current belief systems should be welcomed and examined as a gift from the universal intelligence.

When you go on a diet, at first it feels really hard to resist eating impulsively, but eventually, it gets easier. The same is true with making more elegant choices. At first it feels hard to resist the impulse to express your default response, but over time, it gets easier and feels much better. Kent had to give up spontaneously making what he thought would be witty remarks (which often felt more hurtful than witty to the other person). He worried about becoming dull, boring, and uninteresting if he gave up this personality trait. What he found out was that people liked him a lot more! He had to really care for people without the voice in his head warning him that he would become a wimpy church lady if he suspended expressing his cleverness.

What you need to give up in order to make more elegant choices may be different than what Kent had to give up. Most people are more serious—less irresponsibly playful—than he is, but it's important that you find out what your particular habits are that are keeping you from making elegant choices. It might be the need to be right or to be control or to look good. Or it might be the need to be brighter, smarter, more important. We all have addictive behaviors that feed our egos' needs in lieu of being more magnanimous.

Taking the Higher Road

We are immersed in a culture of consumption and pleasure. The attitude is, if it feels good, do it. Rather than taking full responsibility for our own shortcomings, we blame and project our "shadows" onto others, avoiding the need to look at ourselves honestly. Self-discipline and self-mastery are rare. We know how difficult it is to push ourselves outside our comfort zones, be they physical or emotional. We can feel ourselves marching to the beat of societal norms rather than our own internal drummers, even though intellectually we want to do otherwise. The irony is, because societal conformity is more important than self-authenticity, few of us are truly comfortable in our own skins.

Build your own internal belief system and values. Don't get sucked into collective consciousness (your culture's value system), and if you do, identify it, make another decision, and move on. We are all caught in a double bind: we want approval and recognition from the outside world while at the same time we want to do our own thing. Tony Robbins said, "Nothing tastes as good as healthy feels." Our version of that saying is, the joy of self-mastery far exceeds the pleasure of self-indulgence.

Here in America, it seems that not only are our eyes bigger than our stomachs but our egos are bigger than our brains. We have more confidence than competence. Taking the high road leads to higher results and satisfaction; life just works better at this level. In our case, the higher road was the spiritual road. We wanted to know who we were as spiritual beings having human experiences. We took time to grow up and love ourselves enough that we began to reveal our higher selves. In spite of what you might have heard as a child, you are divine, unique, unconditionally loved, and destined for great things. Why would your Source want anything less for you?

Own Your Own Sh-t

The willingness to accept responsibility for one's own actions is the source from which self-respect springs. Anything that you believe is another's fault (that is, that you blame someone else for) is a measure of how unwilling you are to own your own faulty qualities, which you are projecting on others. And we know from Carl Jung that "everything that irritates us about others can lead us to an understanding of ourselves."

Projection is a psychological term that describes how individuals avoid the pain of owning their own shadows and instead see them as faults in others. This human dynamic is rampant throughout the entire world. Think of the Middle East, where two groups—Jews and Muslims—descended from one prophet (Abraham) have been fighting each other for two thousand years because of the projection of "evil" that they see in each other but not in themselves. What a missed opportunity to create a *we* society based on the teachings of Abraham rather than sinking to sibling rivalry.

Reinvent Yourself—Roles Are Traps

In his early years in the role of parent, Kent believed it was his job to instill his values and beliefs into his kids. He thought father knew best and acted accordingly. Our youngest daughter, Mindy, was very easy going, and she didn't take Dad too seriously. Plus he was okay with the person she was becoming, so they didn't clash that much. There was one issue where there was disagreement: she was still sucking her thumb at night at the age of five or six—too old for her to still be sucking her thumb, or so Kent thought.

As luck would have it, we took this dispute to a Marriage and Family Counselor who immediately took Mindy's side. She looked at Mindy and said, "I want you to take that thumb and suck; suck as much as you want." Then she looked at Kent and said, "This is your problem, and I want you to stop objecting immediately. Next problem?" It was just that fast and that clear. So, Kent backed off, and within a week or so Mindy had completely stopped sucking her thumb. Kent was dumb struck. It was a powerful lesson in "resist not, because what you resist persists."

Our oldest daughter, Molly, on the other hand, was strong willed, had a mind of her own, and often resisted Kent's "coaching," especially during her teenage years. She saw it as controlling and not in her best interest, since it was coming strictly from Kent's own biased point of view. Her independent streak and willingness to go against social convention made him uneasy and concerned that she wouldn't fit in, which was obviously more of a preoccupation for Kent than for her. Truth be told, Kent was willing to give up his essential self to fit in; she was not. He now sees that hers was the elegant choice: "If you want me to be part of your group, I'll do so, but you'll have to take me as I am."

Humans are caught in a catch-22. We fiercely want our independence, but we also want to be accepted, appreciated, and recognized by others. It's a balancing act between these two seeming opposites, and most of us tend to lean one way or the other. Kent was more focused on acceptance, and Molly was more focused on independence. Both extremes can be problematic, because they are both based on ego needs rather than on the highest human behavior that will benefit all in a given situation. Very few of us live with a totally unbiased frame of reference. Somehow we still believe that what is best for the collective is not necessarily best for our individual needs.

In Molly's case, the conflict in her relationship with Kent got so bad that at age fifteen she moved out of our house and stayed with a friend (who Kent thought was too counter-culture) for almost two weeks. She would talk to Marilyn and let her know everything was fine, but she wouldn't speak to Kent. Now that he looks back on it, Kent realizes how brave a thing that was for Molly to do and how bullheaded he must have been that it came to that. Molly went on to graduate magna cum laude from Princeton and received her PhD from Yale, so we hardly had to worry that she might not "fit in."

It's very clear to us now that parenting is not about imposing your values on your children. It's about looking for what your children are meant to become, celebrating that, and encouraging it no matter how dissimilar it may be from your set of values. Khalil Gibran had it right when he said, "Your children are not your children. They are the sons and daughters of Life's longing for itself. They came through you but are not from you and though they are with you, yet they belong not to you."

So You Think You Can Dance

Challenge exists to make things better. Wow, that's a pretty powerful statement. Don't we usually take a different attitude toward challenge? We resist it, curse it, and avoid it. The truth is, all life is change, and all change can be challenging. For some reason, humans prefer the status quo, which never seems to exist for long. In our life experiences, we have come to believe that the evolutionary imperative of our time is to change—and not just any old change. It must be change that creates new virtues, emotional skills, and plain old fashioned wisdom that we did not previously have. A big challenge for Kent was patience. His natural inclination was more to hurry up and push through often without sufficient thought. That never worked well, and it only fed his anxiousness.

The format of the television show *So You Think You Can Dance* is one of our favorite metaphors for how change works in a committed relationship. In the show, two dancers with totally different styles are told to create a new routine together that incorporates the strengths of their individual styles yet is different and unique. Neither of the old styles can dominate. The judges are looking for powerful new dance routines that are better than the individual dancers' original routines.

Before the actual competition, the show will play video of the two dancers in rehearsal, struggling to find that combined style that works for both partners. Both dancers work very hard to make the new routine work; this is not the old ballroom dance routine where the male takes the lead and the woman follows! Sometimes one leads and the other follows and then vice versa. Both contribute; both capitulate. Once the dancers bring their routines to the stage, the judges are looking for a balanced performance and will sometimes give feedback that one partner's style was too dominant or that one partner was not as skilled as the other.

Neither of us are wilting violets, so we have always brought our opinions to our dance routine. Often the issue is whether one opinion should prevail or whether a middle ground is in order. Two heads are better than one, unless one of the heads has too much of a stake in the game, thinking there is too much to lose by compromising. It happens all the time to us, even though we know polarized positions never enhance our "dance routine." Resolving these kinds of situations is where the real work begins. We have a process:

1. We remind ourselves of our foundational goal: to go to higher consciousness together.

2. We acknowledge that in this conflict our lower natures have taken over and that from this place of relative unconsciousness, an elegant resolution is highly unlikely to arise.

3. We agree we're stuck in a catch-22 situation. On the one hand, we want love, adoration, support, and validation from one other. On the other hand, we retain the right to turn on each other, vehemently defending our respective positions (opinions), even at the risk of not being loved, accepted, approved, and adored. It's as if we want to have our cake and eat it too. It's been our experience that we sometimes behave in ways that are not in our own best self-interest! That's crazy, or at least hard to understand. But then, isn't a lot of human behavior hard to understand?

4. We forgive ourselves for being in this dilemma by remembering that, as a species, humans are very young compared to most of the rest of life here on planet Earth. You might say we are still in the adolescent stage as a species, and with some luck, we will not kill ourselves before we mature into more elegant behavior.

5. We need not seek a win/lose or win/win outcome. We have been known to move to one another's points of view and suddenly find ourselves arguing for the exact point we were against a moment earlier. We mutually agree to both walk away from the situation and just let it go, handing the "problem" to a higher prudence. Limited human perspectives can't know everything, so sometimes it is best to trust that there is a higher wisdom that will present itself to resolve every conflict in life situations. Stop resisting, count to ten, and go with the flow, and behold, a resolution will present itself.

This brings us to the word *yield*. Yield has two very different meanings:

1. To give way
2. To give a reward

At first glance, these two definitions may seem to have nothing to do with each other, but we think otherwise. It turns out that in relationships, when you give way, you are rewarded. When you yield your insistence on being right, you yield (sow) love, acceptance, harmony, peace, and intimacy.

Some great scientists report that some of their most significant discoveries came when they gave up, yielded, and admitted they didn't know. In the field of uncertainty (mystery), new information can be revealed, yielding great rewards. So maybe your relationship isn't rocket science, but the principles (universal laws) are the same. Scientist Dr. David Bohm called this the "implicate order."

We don't know everything, but we do know that we have access to an energy field of intelligence that does know. It supports our premise that the goal of our marriage should be to come to higher consciousness together. The secret is to pour out some of what you think you already know, which is currently filling your glass of knowledge, in order to make room for new knowledge to be poured in.

When to Lead and When to Follow

Like it or not, we live in a patriarchal world, and all men have been saturated with a bias toward male superiority and dominance. Kent and Marilyn became young adults in the 1950s, when Father knew best and Mom stayed home, cooked, cleaned, and raised the kids. These were stereotypes we brought into our relationship unknowingly, and even though a half a century has passed, the patriarchal stereotype still exists.

In retrospect, Kent now knows that Marilyn's belief system in the early days of our marriage was a harbinger of things to come: the feminist movement. Kent, on the other hand, showed signs of being an early version of the current-day SNAG—sensitive, new age guy. While we still had to work hard to overcome the influences of patriarchal consciousness, both of us seemed to have shown early signs of a propensity toward gender equality.

On the outside, our relationship looked very much like what we have observed to be the Jewish tradition: the man takes the lead in public, but the woman takes the lead when the family gathers for private prayers and spiritual study. In public Marilyn let Kent be the peacock and pretend he was the boss, while in private, her relationship consciousness ruled the roost. Marilyn admits that her pride wanted more credit in public for her strengths in the relationship, but it was a couple of decades before Kent was comfortable enough in his own skin to allow Marilyn's qualities and skills to go public. Now Kent is more than willing to say that he should have given Marilyn more public acknowledgment from the beginning. For instance, since Marilyn became a minister, he has had to say, "I serve at the pleasure of the minister"–and mean it.

Clarity on gender equality came when we studied Carl Jung, who stated that feminine and masculine traits exist in both genders. Contrary to commonly held beliefs, feminine energy is the more action-oriented energy, and masculine energy is the more passive and contemplative (sometimes degenerating to lazy and self-absorbed). While Kent thought he was the big, macho guy, in fact, he had more trouble surviving in the business world, often changing jobs, than Marilyn, who has used the math and science skills she gained in college effectively and profitably every year for fifty-plus years, either as classroom teacher or as a highly sought-after math tutor.

To our female readers, we say, get used to the fact that your consciousness will lead the way to a more evolved relationship. To the guys, we say, face it; the world is the mess it's in today because men have been running it, so at least entertain the idea that maybe the balance of power needs to shift, both in our committed relationships and in the world.

What Kent finally realized was that he wasn't giving up power by allowing Marilyn more influence in the relationship; he was actually gaining access to powers he alone did not possess. In the end, worrying about who has the power in a committed relationship is futile, because as Ralph Waldo Emerson said, "Nothing external to you has any power over you." Only self-image was at stake, and Kent soon came to realize that Marilyn's good insights, intuitions, and level head were of far greater value than his own puffed-up image of a self-made man that needed nobody's help.

A few months before we were married, Kent and a best friend were having some difficulty installing curtains in our new apartment. Marilyn entered the room, took one look, and offered up a suggestion to resolve the problem. In a heartbeat, Kent's friend threw down his screwdriver in anger and exited the room while yelling over his should, "I'm glad you're marrying her and not me." Marilyn registered immediately what had happened, but she remained silent for a week or two before she brought the subject up with Kent. In spite of the strong patriarchal energy that had been thrown at her, she needed to claim her own identity in the situation. She wanted to know if Kent felt the same as his friend and if she would be expected to keep her opinions to herself in this relationship. Much to her relief, he said, "Absolutely not." One of the things he loved about her was her strength and her independence. And that has never changed in our fifty-plus years together.

Being "hen-pecked" by your wife was a big deal among young men in the 1960s, and Kent was well aware of this. More than once he felt uncomfortable having to tell his drinking buddies after work that it was time to go home to Marilyn and assume his share of the domestic chores and parenting. Kent's own mother had never spoken up for herself to her husband, so like many men, Kent had not seen a model for the marriage partner that life was calling him to become. Fortunately, Marilyn had seen such a relationship in her parents, and she brought that knowledge into ours.

Dear female readers, please don't let this puff you all up; and male readers, don't throw down the book in disgust. Few adults—male or female—have ever experienced a marriage relationship of the type we are talking about in this book. Your current belief system about committed relationships has been strongly influenced by your parents and society at large, which, as we've said, has a patriarchal bias. This is not about shifting the balance of power from patriarch to matriarch. We are attempting to create new relationship paradigm based on equality of gender, which can make every marriage full of adventure and possibility.

Working from the Inside Out

Bible scholars tell us that the historical Jesus said, "The kingdom of God is within." Most people over the past two thousand years have not paid much attention to this teaching. We believe heaven and hell are not some external places we get sent based on the qualities of our lives on earth. Heaven and hell are metaphors for our lives now, and they are of our own making. Everything in our external lives—people, circumstances, events are effect, not cause. They are history, not possibility. Yet we focus on them as if our lives depended upon it, all the while ignoring where all source, all possibility, and all well-being actually resides: within, as Jesus taught. All choice resides within. The choice is to accept what's happening in the external world without objection or attempts to control or manipulate. Yet we try over and over again, thinking our well-being is dependent on external circumstances, people, and events.

Here's how this is important in relationships: Every disharmony in a relationship stems from the mistaken perception that we can manipulate and control anything external to ourselves. The baby has already spilled the milk, yet we choose to get angry, as if that could change anything. Our life partner has already spoken or acted in a way uncongenial to us, yet we choose to be hurt or to object, as if our objection could change what has already occurred.

If you are in an objecting frame of mind, you are a prisoner of your own belief system, unable to see what other life-affirming options might be available to you in the moment. Every human has a yes/no switch. When it's switched to *no*, goes somewhere else, looking for someone who has his or her *yes* switch turned on. In every situation, *yes* is the only answer. If we are expressions of the Source that created us and that Source always says yes, then how can we be any different? Our switch should always be turned to yes.

Most people don't have strong wills; they have strong wonts! It may appear as if we have free will, but in our experience, we really have only one choice—to align ourselves with Life, say yes to what is happening, and find ways to work (dance) with life as it unfolds. Saying no instead is like swimming upstream, which only causes pain and suffering.

This has certainly been our experience in our marriage relationship. Once Kent figured out that Father doesn't know best and that Marilyn had some damn good ideas, our dance together got much better. Our mutual respect and trust grew, as did our interest in each other. As trite as it may seem, we were discovering that two heads really are better than one. Kent usually relied on his rational mental processes and discovered that Marilyn's strong intuitive nature could be of great benefit to him, even in Kent's business life, of which Marilyn had only second-hand knowledge. Her intuitive sense didn't need to be present at his job for her to have some strong, intuitive advice to give Kent about how he could improve things at work. Ugh, was that a bitter pill for him to swallow.

Kent can remember thinking, *How the hell can she have the audacity to give me advice when she has never been in business and doesn't know a thing about the politics at the company?* Intuition wasn't a sense that Kent gave much credence in his earlier years, so he dismissed it as "froufrou."

As modern scientists reveal that we (life) are way more complex than we could ever imagine, we believe it is important to stay open at the top. Don't default to "my mind's made up; don't confuse me with the facts." Be more willing to say, "I don't know." What we have yet to discover is way more interesting than what we already know (or think we know). In relationships, the question is, do you want to be right, or do you want to be in relationship?" In this way, our relationship is always unfolding and creating new experiences.

You Can't Have Anything You Want

The very act of wanting requires a belief that you don't already have everything you need. It is the wanting itself that destroys the possibility of ever having what you want, for the wanting confirms the very lack that you are trying to overcome. Wanting means you believe you are lacking. You try to use the wanting mechanism to put an end to lack, but it's not possible. Wanting implies that something can be possessed, but only spirit is eternal. Everything else is finite and will eventually dissolve. Better to accept what is and remain open to the universe's desire to give you more.

There is only this, only what's happening now, only the present appearance of everything, and this can never be captured, because it is not a thing amongst other things but rather the open, spacious possibility of all possibilities that gives rise to all things in the first place. It cannot be captured because it is not an *it*. If we are honest, we don't really want what we want. What we really want is an end to our wanting. But here's the problem: wanting an end to wanting is another want, perhaps the biggest want of them all!

The wanting obscures the obvious—that we already have everything we could ever want, because right now, an end to all our wants, all our seeking, and all our problems is already within us. Our desires, problems, wants, troubles, and annoyances do not really exist. They are simply thoughts arising now. Here again we have to remember the power of our thoughts to create our own realities or nonrealities, depending on how much control we have over our thinking. If our thoughts are coming from the incorrect beliefs we created in the first few years of our lives, then they may cause us not to see clearly how much abundance would be available to us if our thinking were free of childhood misbeliefs.

We've never seen a relationship where both partners didn't want something from each other, be it for the other person to change, to love him or her more, to share the workload—the list is endless. So how can we be telling you that you can't have *anything* you want? At the end of the day, what is wanting but control? We really want to control the other person, the circumstance, or the outcome. But we can't have control, either. The only things we control are our own attitudes, responses, and behaviors, which is to say, you can control your want to control. Stop wanting to control, and you'll get what you really want: Equanimity! Peace!

You don't lack anything. You don't need anything. The only reason you don't know and experience this in your everyday life is that you don't understand what your only source for everything, visible and invisible, is: God. God is always giving, and it is our job to always respond with an unconditional *yes* to ever new challenge God/life has to give us.

You may have to spend some serious time in silent contemplation of what you just read, because chances are, your rational mind will never totally get it. Ultimately, the only way to truly "get it" is from a deep, silent place within—not through the rational mind, but from the heart of your intuition. The universe is already giving you everything you need; the problem is that you're too unaware to receive it. If you can assimilate and absorb a deep knowledge of this, you will put an end to your wanting. The Buddhists call this *mindfulness*, ironically meaning conscious awakeness not rational thinking.

Unto ourselves, we are nothing and can do nothing. But once we deeply understand who we are, we realize that we are conduits for love in the universe. We can't do what the universe can do, but we can be clear channels through which the qualities of the universe are made manifest on the physical plane.

This brings us back to the purpose of marriage, as defined earlier by Ram Dass. A marriage relationship is a laboratory in which two people can fully realize and express their true natures as clear channels of expression through which the universe can reveal its highest essence. And you thought marriage was just about copulation and companionship!

You Don't Know What You Know

Any place where your mind is made up is a place where a deeper knowledge cannot penetrate. In the name of self-confidence and individuality, we project a bravado or shyness that keeps us safe— perhaps even admired and respected—but, as we said earlier, it also causes us to fall into the trap of thinking: *My mind's made up; don't confuse me with the facts.*

Intentionally moving to a place of uncertainty feels absolutely life threatening. Dropping all sense of self-assuredness is like peeling off our own skin; that's how attached we are to our opinions, behaviors, and self-identities. And it's even tougher when it means totally capitulating to the opinion or feedback of your significant other. Seriously entertaining the possibility that your partner sees things more clearly than you do can be a huge struggle. For sure you can see he or she sees differently.

In our relationship, Kent had the most trouble with staying open to the possibility that Marilyn was right. Perhaps males are more susceptible to the powerful need to be right. For both of us, this need comes from someplace deep in the unconscious. Ironically, sometimes our survival instincts can run counter to our own best self-interest.

Wrestling with this deep, self-righteous power is critically important, not just because your relationship with your partner will benefit, but because total surrender of the little self is the key to having a viable relationship with the Higher Self. We need only look at the condition of humankind on the planet today to see that our little wills are so completely out of control that the continuation of our species is at stake.

There is much truth in the hymn that says, "Let there be peace on earth, and let it begin with me." Where else could it begin? This also applies to our most intimate relationships: let there be peace in our marriage/partnership, and let it begin with me. As long as we hold on to our own points of view and object to those of others, there cannot be peace in our relationships.

It's one thing to make the intellectual decision to live a more conscious life; it's quite another to execute it. We are hardwired with a gaggle of half-baked opinions, beliefs, and self-important notions that are very hard to overcome. They're called our egos, our stories, or our personalities. We think they are who we are, but they are not. Ego stands for **E**dging **G**od **O**ut. Letting go of who you think you are is tough, and it really helps to have a loving life companion who can coach you. But you have to be willing to accept the coaching. Since the ego wants to protect itself at all cost, it will resist all attempts at dethroning it. Coming to realize that we both had skills, intuitions, and insights the other did not was both difficult and liberating. We didn't have to do it all—know it all—alone. The very act of capitulating to each other's coaching was a big step in becoming responsible for manifesting more conscious behavior.

If you don't love yourself, how can others love you? Be the loving, nonjudgmental support the other needs to get healthy. Self-love first; then you can be free to love another without attachments. Be as transparent to each other as possible. Be open to the other being your teacher. Ask the other for help. Use the strengths the other has that you don't have and vice versa.

Humility is one of the highest human values, and few of us manifest it adequately. It is the gateway to building a meaningful life and a lasting relationship with another human being. It's going to feel like crucifixion at first, but all that is dying is your self-important ego.

What's being birthed is not a self at all; it's a clarity of consciousness that allows the larger Self to express through you.

Staying in the "Forever Just" Moment

Can you remember sometime in your life when you felt euphoric—maybe for just a moment or perhaps as long as a year or more? For us, getting married was a euphoric moment, and the feeling lingered for quite a long time. Some people call it the honeymoon phase of marriage, and when it ends, it can be replaced by regret, longing, or "wishing for." People can then move to a condition of wanting the past to return or the future to be better than the present.

The Buddha had this to say on the subject: "Do not dwell in the past. Do not dream of the future. Concentrate the mind on the present moment." Very early in our marriage, we decided we wanted our lives together to always be just like the initial marriage euphoria, rather than getting old, stale, and repetitive. So, we set our intention to be "forever just married."

Let us quickly admit that we have not always stayed in the "forever just married" zone. When we are not in the zone, it's sort of like a mini-divorce, which required us to develop another strategy. "Divorce" is okay as long as you quickly recommit.

Somewhere along the way, we were given this advice: never go to bed mad or with a conflict unresolved. Even if you have to stay up all night, get it resolved and move on. There were times when Kent wanted to roll over and go to sleep, but to Marilyn's credit, she forced us to hang in there until we were "remarried."

You don't have to hang on to resentment or anger. Or if you do, absolutely make it for less than twenty-four hours! Staying mad is like keeping your fist clenched when someone is trying to put a

$1,000 bill in it. Sooner or later, we all have to get over our anger and resolve things, so why not make it sooner. We've heard stories of siblings or parents and children who held on to resentment for fifty years or more. What's the point of that? How many $1,000 bills slipped away because they wouldn't open their hands?

Some people seem to think that "giving in" is settling for something less than what they want. We found that giving in actually produced something better than what we thought we wanted individually. "The more the sacrifice, the more the reward," would be one way to put it. But then again, sacrifice (and surrender) seem to be very uncongenial to people. They would rather be miserable and "right" than happy and in relationship. As you've read in this book, you've probably found that gaining control over your self-centered ego is a major theme. In fact, it's probably the single most important ingredient in our relationship. There's more to life than just getting your way all the time. As the old American Indian fable goes, there are two wolves wrestling inside each of us (the lower self and the higher self), and the one you feed is the one that wins.

CHAPTER 9

The Confluence of Science and Spirit

Science is not only compatible with spirituality;
it is a profound source of spirituality.
—Carl Sagan, astronomer, cosmologist,
astrophysicist, and astrobiologist

The pursuit of scientific understanding of the nature of the universe began in the sixteenth century with philosophers and thinkers like Galileo Galilei. This approach to understanding life immediately met strong resistance from the Catholic Church, which believed it was the ultimate authority on the interpretation of life. This conflict continued for several centuries until the evidence was so overwhelming that the scientific pursuit had to be given an equal stance in the public discourse—separate but equal.

By the 1900s, new spiritual teachers had come on the scene with different perspectives on the expression of God. Among these perspectives was that of Christian Science, which was founded by Mary Baker Eddy, an early advocate of transcendental meditation, theosophy, and new thought. Rather than call themselves "religions," such schools of thought chose to be called "spiritual" or "metaphysical" movements. This trend has continued to the current day, when more Americans call themselves spiritual than religious. These new spiritual movements emphasized the laws of the universe, as defined by modern day scientists, rather than the experiences of a few ancient enlightened beings, which were often recorded many years after the fact by people who were not present at the actual events.

In the last hundred years or so, some of the smartest people in the history of mankind have devoted their lives to breakthrough research in physics, mathematics, neuroscience, and the nature of consciousness. In our opinion this research is moving us closer to the awe and mystery of life that religions have been talking about for centuries.

The good news about this is that the masses of atheists, agnostics, and other skeptics now have a new doorway into understanding the mysteries of the universe and their place in it. If the word *God* doesn't work for you, you now have the option to use *universal consciousness, the implicate order, creative source, energetic fields of information, pure potentiality*, or whatever you like.

This brings us to the word *confluence*, which means "a coming/ flowing together, meeting, or gathering at one point." We've spent a lifetime studying religions of the West and the East (including the teachings of Jesus of Nazareth and Lao Tzu); participating in the Human Potential movement in the 1970s and '80s; studying the field of self-realization, founded by Paramahansa Yogananda; investigating a new thought philosophy known as the Science of Mind, as propounded in a book of the same name by Ernest Holmes; and absorbing the contributions of scientists such as David Bohm, Albert Einstein, Dr. Jose Dispenza, and Dr. Andrew Newberg. After all this, we have come to the conclusion that we like to hang out in the "confluence." We have tried to write a book informed by the confluence of all the experience and knowledge we've gained over the last fifty-plus years.

Whether you are Christian, Jew, Hindu, Muslim, or a twenty-first-century rationalist, there's something in this book for you. Just remember, a glass already full of water can receive no more water. Just as you can never step in the same stream twice, if you take today's beliefs into tomorrow, you run the risk of letting the stream of consciousness pass you by. Love is a verb, not a noun, and we are human becomings, not static beings. If you already know what you're looking for, you'll never have the experience of discovering something brand new.

Your Emotional Guidance System

The Abraham-Hicks Emotional Guidance Scale lets you know if you're directing your life toward pain or toward pleasure. Just as a smoke detector's beeping warns you that its batteries are low, so negative emotion is an indication that your connection to Source Energy is weak, that you're headed away from pleasure and toward pain. The purpose of emotion is to give you feedback about the vibrational content of your thoughts. This is crucial information because the vibrational content of your thoughts determines what you are attracting and creating.

The feedback we receive from our emotions is similar to the feedback we get when we touch a hot stove. Although we appreciate the warning from a hot stove, most of us have been trained to undervalue the information we receive from our emotions. Negative emotion is a warning that redirection is in order—that we're headed toward something we do not want. By referring to the list below, you can determine your current emotional status.

Abraham – Hicks Emotional Guidance System (listed in order from most pleasure to most pain)

Joy/Agape Love
Passion
Enthusiasm/Eagerness/Happiness
Positive Expectation/Belief
Optimism
Hope
Contentment
Boredom
Pessimism
Frustration/Irritation/Impatience
Overwhelm
Disappointment
Doubtfulness
Worry
Blame
Discouragement
Anger
Revengeful
Hatefulness/Rage
Jealousy
Insecurity/ Guilt/Unworthiness
Fear/Grief/Depression/Despair/Powerlessness

Do you remember the children's board game Chutes and Ladders? It applies perfectly to the Emotional Guidance Scale. Imagine a ladder going up from the bottom of the scale and a chute coming down from the top. Choose a positive thought, and you'll climb the ladder. As you climb the ladder, you'll feel more well-being. You'll be more empowered. You'll attract more of what you want. Choose a negative thought, and you'll slide down the chute. On your way down, your connection to Source Energy will be weakened. You'll feel powerless and befuddled. You'll attract people and things you don't want in your life.

With an understanding of your emotional guidance system, it becomes clear when you choose a thought that zooms you up the ladder and just as clear when you choose a thought that sends you down the chute. Feel-good thoughts are ladders that raise your emotional vibration, just as feel-bad thoughts are chutes that lower your vibration.

To climb the ladder toward empowerment and away from powerlessness, monitor how you feel and then choose a thought that feels better. If you have a clear understanding of your emotional guidance system, when you feel bad, you'll always have an option to feel better. You can always climb the ladder by choosing a thought that takes you up the scale.

If you get sideswiped by some event and take a fast ride down the chute, the best response is to look for a ladder on which to climb back up. Look for a thought that feels better than the way you feel currently and deliberately guide your thoughts toward what feels better. Each time you choose a thought that feels even a little better, you'll climb up another rung of the emotional scale, and soon you will be back where you want to be. When you hit bottom emotionally, you can either freak out and pretend you're powerless, or you can take back your power by choosing thoughts that feel better.

Just keep climbing the ladder, and you'll be back in alignment— feeling joyful, empowered, and appreciative. As you continue climbing the emotional scale, you will enjoy the supreme confidence of knowing that you are truly the master creator of your own life! As you continue choosing thoughts that feel better, you will *know* with certainty that you can be and do and have and feel whatever you choose! Victor Frankl, Holocaust survivor and author, said it this way: "Everything can be taken from a man but one thing: the last of the human freedoms—to choose one's attitude in any given set of circumstances, to choose one's own way."

How to Walk through Life as a Modern Mystic

A mystic is defined as "a person who seeks by contemplation and self-surrender to obtain unity with or absorption into the Deity or the absolute, or who believes in the spiritual apprehension of truths that are beyond the intellect." We're suggesting here that we are all being asked to become modern mystics. We are being called to walk through life in deep reverence and awareness of our oneness with all. The great spiritual master, Jesus of Nazareth, knew this truth two thousand years ago, and his teachings are still available for those who "have ears to hear and eyes to see." He said that we would someday do the same things as him, only greater. Do we dare to take him at his word and see ourselves as capable of the depth of his divine realization?

Modern mystics of the last two hundred years have enhanced our own understanding of the mystical way—people such as Mathew Fox, Joel Goldsmith, Michael Bernard Beckwith, Andrew Harvey, Evelyn Underhill, Ernest Holmes, Mary Baker Eddy, Eckhart Tolle, Wayne Dyer, Thich Nhat Hahn, Ghandi, and Mother Teresa and many more. These mystics teach that we should see this world as divine, given to us to steward in a way that leads to peace, communal prosperity, health, and justice. It is a path based on seeing ourselves as one sacred family. It is a path of blessing and wholeness and sacred embodiment of the feminine and masculine principles in harmony.

According to the great evolutionary mystics throughout the ages, the ultimate purpose of evolution is to bring heaven to earth and birth the God in man that is waiting to be revealed. That is what awaits us at the end of our hero's journey as modern mystics.

The Nature of the Universe

So, fifty-plus years after our relationship began, here we are with more than enough knowledge and personal experience to have an opinion about the nature of the universe, and we do! It goes like this:

Approximately 13.5 billion years ago, before anything had manifested in the universe, there still was something. It was invisible, but it was powerful beyond belief. Everything we see and know about the universe today was superconcentrated in one spot 13.5 billion years ago. All the matter, all the potential, and all the energy that has unfolded over the last fourteen billion years was waiting to become, and become it did. We call that the original Big Bang.

Out of that bang came everything that has existed or still does exist, including you and me. We are currently the highest form of intelligence and consciousness we know of as a result of the original bang. Here's the problem with language: when we say *a result of*, the mind (yours and mine) thinks of that result as being separate from the bang itself—and that's just not true. The original bang is still becoming, and so are we. Whatever cosmic intelligence creates, sustains, guides, and directs all future becoming is pushing everything, including us, to higher and higher potentials. Much of the nature around us may already be at its highest potential, but humankind is not.

We are still becoming. We still have lots more potential to reveal and manifest. The energy or power we call *life force* is in every one of our one hundred trillion cells, and they are all saying, "There's more for you; you're not complete. Wake up and pay attention, and the "more" will be revealed to you." Thus comes the thought that "humans are sleepwalking in a dream state, totally cocooned by belief systems that have been passed down unconsciously from generation to generation." These faulty belief systems include one that has greatly disserved us—that there is a anthropomorphic "God" behind it all. We even refer to this God as *He*!

Don't get us wrong, *God* is a handy three-letter word to describe the mystery, the intelligence, and the benevolence of the universe, but unfortunately the word *God* is also loaded with lots of baggage in the minds of the billions of people who use it—including us. The true god of the universe cannot be reduced to a single word; it can only be experienced, known at a very deep level within, creating a deep conviction that can't be reduced to words.

Consider this first verse of the Jonathan Star translation of the Tao Te Ching, the most comprehensive text on the Tao by Lao Tzu:

A way that can be walked
is not The way,
A name that can be named
is not The Name

Tao is both Named and
Nameless
As Nameless, it is the origin of
all things
As Named, it is the mother of
all things

A mind free of thought,
merged within itself,
beholds the essence of Tao
A mind filled with thought,
identified with its own
perceptions,
beholds the mere forms of this
world

Tao and this world seem
different
but in truth they are one and
the same
The only difference is in what
we call them

How deep and mysterious is
this unity
How profound, how great!
It is the truth beyond the truth,
the hidden within the hidden
It is the path to all wonder,
the gate to the essence of
everything!

Chapter 10

Changing Your Beliefs

*The concept of the Divine Matrix as a universally connected hologram
promises us that we're limited only by our beliefs. As the ancient
spiritual traditions suggest, the invisible walls of our deepest beliefs
can become our greatest prisons. Yet they also remind us that it's our
beliefs that can become our greatest source of freedom. As different as
the world's wisdom traditions may be from one another, they all bring
us to the same conclusion: the opportunity to be imprisoned or free is
ours, and we're the only ones who can make the choice.*
—from *The Divine Matrix* by Greg Braden

Behind every feeling of frustration, anger, fear, disappointment,
depression, remorse, and more is a false belief. Somewhere in your
early life, you made a decision (lots of them, in fact) that you thought
was necessary at the time. Through repeated use, these decisions
have become part of your belief system, and they are currently
running your life—for better or worse.

At the time, those decisions seemed logical, and perhaps it seemed
you had only one choice. At times, your choices worked. But as an
adult, you have an opportunity to rethink those choices that did not
work and intentionally eliminate them from your conscious habits.

In the process, you will allow more productive beliefs to emerge. Changing your old, conditioned responses can shift your life from hit or miss to a more intentional, consistent experience of success.

Here's what you do:

1. Identify a current belief that you know is no longer serving you.
2. Ask your higher self how you might change this belief into one that does serve you.
3. Create a list of the pros and cons for your current belief as well as for your new choice.

Write your current belief here: _____

_____

_____

List the strengths and weaknesses of this belief.

Pros	Cons

Write your optional new belief here: _____

_____

_____

List the strengths and weaknesses of this new belief.

Pros	Cons

Now visualize this new belief coming from your higher self to your mind, permanently embedding itself there as a replacement for the old belief that no longer serves you. Follow these steps:

1. Declare your understanding of the One Mind. (For instance, it's all there is.)
2. Recognize your connection to the One Mind. (You and the One Mind are one.)
3. State your intention to eliminate the old belief. (Feel the fire in your belly.)
4. Realize that you can choose to make the new belief a reality in your state of being.
5. Express your gratitude for this process.
6. Release your word into the law of the One Mind.

How to Connect Deeply with Another Who Doesn't Agree with You

1. Invite cooperation from the beginning when raising an issue. Say, "I know we disagree on this issue, and I would

like to find a way to resolve our disagreement." Do this with a spirit of goodwill.

2. Listen to the other with a view to understanding, not agreement or disagreement. Don't try to win the debate, convince others of your rightness, or convert them to another point of view.

3. Stay absolutely present. Practice mindfulness. Keep your attention focused, and don't begin formulating your response when the other person is still speaking. Allow a pause before responding. Think about your response twice before verbalizing it.

4. Identify and explore the other person's core values and interests, underlying hopes, needs, concerns, motivations, fears, and ideals. See where your values are the same and where they are different. Allow that to be okay.

5. Separate the other person's suggested solutions for satisfying the core interests from the interests themselves. Don't dismiss a good idea just because it is coming from someone you don't like, trust, or respect.

6. Reveal the backstory of why you believe what you believe. Sharing deeply invites deep understanding and connection.

7. When disagreements occur, listen harder. You'll often find that the problem is a gap in your knowledge of the events in the other person's life that have led him or her to that position.

8. Work together on an agreement that meets both your interests—as much as possible. Again, ask, "How can we come to a mutually acceptable solution to our disagreement?"

9. It may be that you'll discover an apology is needed on one side or the other for past wrongs. Be vulnerable and willing.

Traits Found in Successful Long-Term Relationships
(Source: *If the Buddha Married* by Charlotte Kasl, PhD)

- a strong liking for or attraction to each other, often from the moment they met; many said they became "best friends"
- a deep level of commitment to being a couple as well as separate individuals
- an ability to resolve conflicts
- shared values, dreams, and lifestyles
- showing appreciation, respect, care, and consideration for each other
- taking pleasure and delight in each other's company
- a capacity to pull together during hard times
- strong connections to community and a commitment to being of service to others
- a good sense of humor and an ability to laugh at and reflect on themselves
- supporting each other to be their best self

Still Going Strong

After thirty-one years living in southern California, we moved north to San Jose, near one daughter, one son-in-law, two grandkids, and San Francisco, where Marilyn's family is from. We joined a Center for Spiritual Living, which is a new thought, nondenominational faith tradition that was started in Los Angeles in 1927 by a brilliant metaphysician and author, Ernest Holmes. After taking several qualifying classes, Marilyn enrolled in practitioner training and became a certified RScP, or Religious Science Practitioner. Four years later, Kent followed in her footsteps.

But the universal plan for Marilyn wasn't finished yet. In 2008, she was "called" to attend the ministerial school at Agape International Spiritual Center, the founder and senior spiritual director of which is Rev. Dr. Michael Bernard Beckwith. It required Marilyn to fly from San Jose to LA once a week, 33 weeks a year, for four years, which she did. In 2012, she earned her master's in consciousness studies and became an official Agape-trained minister. While in school, she started her own ministry called Heart Space Teachings, an omnifaith, nondenominational spiritual community, here in San Jose.

That's when the fun of a working relationship really paid off. Kent gladly joined her in this new life direction. Kent became the minister's husband. Today we have a successful spiritual organization—we don't like to call it a "church," because we believe that is a word from the old religious paradigm. We're a teaching institution with a spiritual bent that also teaches the research of quantum physicists, who are redefining the nature of consciousness in a way that we metaphysicians can agree with. For the first time since Galileo in the 1500s, science and spirituality are in agreement about the nature of life.

Here we are, on the bleeding edge of the evolutionary force that never gives up on life as we know it here on planet Earth. Sometimes it looks like a matter of life and death, and it may be. But all we can do is put all our energy, thought, and effort on the side of life, for we absolutely believe the imperative at this time is to wake up as humans, see the truth of the larger reality in which we exist, and get on board. Let the river of life take us where it will, because we know it will be in our best interest as a species. It's the grandest adventure of our life yet, and we're totally up for it. We invite you to join us.

ABOUT KENT AND MARILYN

Rev. Marilyn and Kent Pelz cofounded Heart Space Teachings in 2010 as a nondenominational, new thought/ageless wisdom spiritual community. They believe that in this age of the rational mind, the power of the heart can be overlooked. The heart is the empress of the body and the gateway to the mystical. The magnetic field of the heart exceeds that of the brain by five thousand times. The Heart Space Teachings community emanates from this magnetic force field.

Marilyn has an MS in Consciousness Studies from Agape International Spiritual Center, and Kent is a spiritual counselor.

The source of their teachings is the new thought and ageless wisdom brought into the light by spiritual masters throughout the ages: Buddha, Jesus, Saint Teresa of Avila, Ernest Holmes, Michael Bernard Beckwith, Oprah, Wayne Dyer. Eckhart Tolle, Deepak Chopra, and many, many more.

We don't ask you to park your brain at the door, but we do ask you to consider the expression "Don't trust everything your mind tells you." The New Thought philosophy combines science and spirit, drawing the best from both approaches to understand Reality with a capital R, remaining open to the certainty that there's more to come.

Printed in the United States
By Bookmasters